W9-BNR-365

Mommy! I Have to Go Potty!

2nd Edition

Mommy! I Have to Go Potty!

A Parent's Guide to Toilet Training

FULLY REVISED AND EXPANDED

R&R
Raefield-Roberts, Publishers

By Jan Faull, M.Ed.

Updated and Expanded by Helen F. Neville, B.S., R.N.

Illustrations by Rebekah Trusty • Foreword by Helen F. Neville

Text and charts copyright © 2009, by Jan Faull
Illustrations copyright © 2009, by Raefield-Roberts, Publishers

All rights reserved

First edition, 1996
Second edition, 2009

Revised and Expanded by Helen F. Neville, B.S., R.N.
Cover and interior design by Judy Petry
Cover illustration by Rebekah Trusty
Printed in the United States of America

ISBN 978-0-9650477-1-5
Library of Congress Control number 2008937634

Co-published by:
Raefield-Roberts, Publishers
10214 183 Ave. E.
Bonney Lake, WA 98391
and
Parenting Press, Inc.
P.O. Box 75267
Seattle, WA 98175

*To see all our helpful publications and services for parents, caregivers,
and children, to go www.ParentingPress.com*

Contents

Foreword

From my experience as a parent, I know toilet training is a very individual matter. Our firstborn was a strong-minded perfectionist. Having heard about the risks of toilet-training power struggles, I knew I didn't want to go there. So, although I bought a potty chair sometime after our son turned two, we all ignored it. A few months after he turned three, the time felt right to start training. So I began each morning by asking if he wanted to wear diapers or big boy underpants that day. Some days he chose one, some days the other. Within a few weeks the switch was complete, without a single accident. It was smooth, easy, and well worth the wait.

I planned to use the same approach for our second-born. To my amazement, at 17 months she toddled up to her brother's potty chair and tugged her diaper off. Within days, she was in panties full-time. However, when she turned 28 months, we moved and I returned to work. She returned to diapers full-time and continued to be in them for a number of months. Individual differences, physical and emotional readiness, as well as family circumstances all contribute to the mix.

My new job was that of pediatric advice nurse, advising parents about illness, immunizations, behavior, and development—including toilet training. No one ever called to report toilet training success. Parents called about resistance. Given the risks of flaring tempers and backed up bowels, the best advice was always to step back and offer more time for this child to grow into readiness.

My role at work expanded to include counseling parents about differences in inborn temperament. The consideration of temperament added an entirely new dimension to my understanding of toilet training.

For example, cautious kids need more time to get comfortable with new bathroom equipment. Children who find transitions difficult need extra time to prepare for and make the big change from diapers to using the toilet. Kids with low sensitivity to body signals won't notice the urge to go until it's *strong*, which, as a consequence, leaves little time to get to the bathroom. Inborn traits call for parental attention and creativity.

Having written several books for parents, I was delighted when asked to update and expand Jan Faull's *Mommy! I Have to Go Potty!* which has been a valuable guide to toilet training since its original release in 1996. Children's varied development, individual time tables, and unique reactions to toilet training have not changed. However, many other things *have* changed: new equipment, greater numbers of children in child care; a growing concern for the environment; as well as increased awareness of temperament and diversity. To reflect these changes, relevant updates have been made throughout the text and three new chapters have been added on child care, special needs, and very early potty training (which is common throughout much of the world).

Mommy! I Have to Go Potty! includes many different approaches to toilet training. As I'd learned from personal experience, techniques that worked with one child may need altering for a second child who has his or her own pace of development and unique temperament. Sometimes there are also differences of opinion between generations. Every mother, father, child care provider, or grandparent who has toilet trained a child has advice on how to proceed. Your job is to find what works well for your child and your family. This book will help you to do just that.

—Helen F. Neville, B.S., R.N.
Author of Is *This a Phase?* and *Temperament Tools*

Introduction

Successful **toilet training—that is,** training completed with as little emotional upheaval as possible, in a time frame attuned to the child—requires a blend of techniques on the part of the parent and readiness on the part of the child. This book will show you how to familiarize your child with using the toilet so that readiness, interest, and willingness all come together. Each child learns to use the toilet in a unique way.

Most children are successfully trained by the age of three and a half. For some, training happens easily, for others, many accidents and power plays between parent and child occur along the way. Each child has his own time frame for training. The parent's job is to determine when his readiness alarm goes off and guide him to toileting success. For some children the alarm is loud and clear; you know exactly when they're ready. For others, it's more like a snooze alarm—the child wakes up to the idea of learning use the toilet, but keeps drifting back to sleep, and needs waking up again and again.

No matter how you approach guiding your child to use the toilet, there are three points to keep in mind before you get started. First, anyone training a child needs to show respect for the child's most private body parts and proceed in a respectful manner. If parents yell, hit, express frustration, or act disgusted, children may develop negative associations with toileting. Urinating and having a bowel movement are natural and necessary parts of everyone's day. We all eat, sleep, and eliminate. We want children to have pleasant associations with this natural process. So stay positive and pleasant during toilet training.

Second, cultivate your child's interest in using the toilet. If your child senses this activity is mostly for your benefit, she might balk. Don't make toilet training more important to you than it is to your child. If you're doubtful about how to proceed, it's usually better to do less rather than more. Always remember that ultimate control lies with your child.

Third, as you proceed with toilet training, don't let the process dominate your relationship. Yes, it's important, but you still need to read stories, play, and talk with your child about topics unrelated to toileting.

So, read on. Gather ideas, keep in mind your child's uniqueness, and develop a plan that works for both of you.

—Jan Faull

1

Is It Time Yet?

Just as children eventually learn behaviors like sitting at the table to eat, or sleeping through the night, and skills such as reading, or bike riding, children learn to use the toilet. Most of them do this between the ages of two and three and a half years old. In general, if your child hasn't made any progress in daytime toilet training by this age, bring it up with your doctor or nurse.

When it comes to guiding children toward a new competency, it's important to choose the right time. We don't teach two year olds to read and we don't train three year olds to ride a two-wheel bicycle. Immature and under-developed bodies and minds are not equipped to learn advanced skills, no matter how qualified the instruction. Education must mesh with a child's developing ability to learn a new task. If a child's physical maturation is out of sync with instruction for toilet training, frustration occurs rather than competence.

On the other hand, don't let the opportunity for learning slip by. If a child's body is ready to learn a new skill, teach it; just don't be too surprised if she objects. Reluctance is a common response to change. Give the child time to adjust to the new learning experience. The newness causes the emotional upheaval; it doesn't mean the child can't learn the skill.

Most seven year olds can learn to swim; most six and a half year olds are ready to learn to read; and most two and a half year olds can begin to learn to use the toilet. If you wait months, or even years longer, children get set in their ways and resist or fear the change that learning a new skill brings.

Knowing or sensing when the time is right for your child to learn a new behavior is a key to effective parenting. Physical maturation of the body is often necessary before a child can master a new skill, but it isn't isolated. A child is more complex. Parents must keep in mind the child's intellectual, social, and emotional development as they train their child to learn the skills required of them in our society.

Toilet training is not an isolated event of simply learning to urinate and have bowel movements in the toilet. The process involves four aspects of your developing child: physical, intellectual, social, and emotional. It's important to understand how each of these areas impacts the child being trained. Using the toilet is much more about learning than about the rote repetition the term "training" usually implies. We use the term toilet training in this book because it is a common cultural term.

PHYSICAL READINESS

Children can't walk until their muscles are developed enough to carry them across the room. They can't write the alphabet until their finger muscles are able to form intricate shapes. A child won't really be successful using the toilet independently until the bowel and bladder muscles are strong and under control.

In order to be toilet trained, these muscles must be developed sufficiently to hold in the urine and stool. For most infants and toddlers in diapers, pee and poop[1] simply come out when the bladder or rectum is full. When a child is physically ready to be toilet trained, the muscles are strong enough to hold the urine and stool in and the child is able to relax and let go when the time is right.

If your child is constantly wet, he simply isn't ready. Notice when your child's diaper is dry for an hour and a half to two hours at a time. This is your first indication that the bladder is growing and its muscles are developing control. Most toddlers pee four to eight times a day.

As your child plays, notice if he stops his activity when he's having a bowel movement. If he does, it is a sign he knows something is happening with his body. Comment, "You're pooping in your diaper. Someday you'll go in the toilet." He isn't ready to use the toilet, but it's

---

[1] In this book you'll see the words "pee" and "poop" used because they are the potty training words most used and easily recognized by children. Some families use the words "wet" and "messy." Use whatever toileting vocabulary is comfortable for your family and understandable to your child's caregivers.

significant that he recognizes what he's doing. If your child actually gets up and walks to his bedroom to have a bowel movement in his diaper, he has developed control of his rectal muscles.

Independent physical readiness includes being able to pull pants down and up. Make sure clothes are easy to manage. A long shirt and a bare bottom when at home can simplify matters even more.

Stories from the Bathroom

Too Early *(Nathan, 2½ years)*

Mom was ready to start educating Nathan to use the toilet. He was willing to sit on the toilet, but never performed. So Mom and Nathan shopped for special superhero underwear. Nathan was excited to wear these underpants. For three days Mom tried training Nathan. He wet his pants hourly. Pee would run down his leg but Nathan would not feel a thing. He just kept playing.

It was clear Nathan had no internal messages about "the need to go." Mom put him back in diapers, but because Nathan insisted on wearing the superhero underpants, she just stretched them over his diapers and waited until his body developed further.

Not Really Ready *(Juliana, 2 years)*

Alma was determined to have Juliana trained by her birthday. Grandma was coming to visit and Alma wanted to show off her skill as a mom and how cooperative her daughter was.

Little Juliana was eager to please. She wore her panties proudly and remained dry, but only peed in the toilet once or twice a day at Alma's request. Mom waited for Juliana to tell her she needed to go, but she didn't. A couple of times a day, Mom would set her on her little toilet seat and tell her to go. Juliana knew how to hold her urine in, but hadn't developed to the point mentally or physically where she could release it when her bladder was full. At night, when Juliana finally relaxed, she wet her bed thoroughly. This set up a pattern that

—continued on next page

—continued from previous page

continued until she was six.

Alma could claim Juliana was trained, but her daughter paid for this early declaration with years of unnecessary bedwetting. If she had waited until Juliana had developed physically just a little bit more, she may have been able to prevent those years of bedwetting.

When you look for signs of physical readiness, it's important to note if your child is over the thrill of learning to walk and run. The sturdy walker or confident runner who now sits on the floor to play with toys will be more willing to sit on the toilet than the child who still wants to practice running.

SOCIAL READINESS

Your next step is to recognize that steering children toward toileting is easier if they participate in it as a social experience. The question for most parents is: How in the world do you make toileting social? Try the following ideas.

First, take your child with you to use the toilet and encourage him to do the flushing. Put a potty chair in the bathroom and when you use the toilet, encourage him to sit on the little potty chair. In the beginning, don't bother taking his diapers off and don't expect any success. Just get him accustomed to sitting on the potty. Talk and enjoy this time together. Be encouraging and say, "Someday you'll use the toilet just like Mom or Dad."

Some children won't want a little potty chair on the floor; they'll want to sit on the big toilet. If this is the case with your child, purchase a potty seat that fits on the big toilet. Encourage your child to set dolls and stuffed animals on the toilet seat to play toileting. (Use a large-enough stuffed animal so that it won't risk clogging the drain if you turn your back for a moment and it falls in.) Through play, children learn about toileting. If the teddy bear accidentally falls in the toilet, calmly rescue him, and allow the play to continue. Your child will learn from this experience that if she falls in, like the teddy, she will be rescued and not flushed away. All of these activities help children warm up to the idea of using the toilet themselves.

Girls have bodies like their moms. They see what she does and they learn from copying her behavior. When dads get involved in training boys, it also helps them succeed. If the same-sex parent isn't involved, a child will still learn to use the toilet, it may just take a little longer.

It really helps if your child can watch another child, who is similar in age, perform on the toilet. This puts toileting in his realm of possibility. He thinks, "If my cousin can do it, I can, too." If there are older brothers and sisters in the house, you can encourage the younger child to watch them in the bathroom (but only with permission from the older child). Remember, children together in the bathroom always need adult supervision.

Modeling by peers is often all it takes for toileting success to occur. For children in a child care setting, social readiness is naturally encouraged since children want to participate in the bathroom activities along with the others.

Stories from the Bathroom

A Friend to Copy *(Jamar, 4 years)*

Jamar was urine trained, but determined not to poop in the toilet. Each night after his bedtime story, he pooped in his diaper and called Mom to clean him up. Then one day when friend Michael came to play, Jamar watched him have a bowel movement in the toilet. Jamar was impressed with Michael's ability and skill. He decided that if Michael, who was his same age and size, could poop in the toilet, so could he. Now Jamar has his bowel movement at bedtime, in the toilet, before his story.

Another sign of social readiness is imitation. Does your child mimic you shaving, cooking, or shopping? If so, he may be ready to imitate toileting practices too. This is a good sign.

INTELLECTUAL READINESS

A positive social bathroom experience increases readiness, but your child also needs to make the connection between his mind and body about "the need to go." This is intellectual readiness.

Some ability to communicate about the process of peeing and pooping is also necessary—be it words, hand signs, or body motions. Children need a toileting vocabulary. It's best to use words, such as pee, poop, urinate, and bowel movement, that are understandable not only to people in your home, but also to teachers, nurses, child care providers, and other parents. Cutesy terms—"si-si" and "uh-uh"—familiar only in your household, won't help your child when she ventures beyond the boundaries of your home.

For your child, intellectual readiness comes in three steps. The first is awareness that she "has gone." The day she indicates with words or body language that her diapers are full, wet, or need changing is an important first step.

The next step is awareness from your child that she "is going" right now. Comments like, "Poop is coming out, Mom" or, "I feel the pee dripping down my leg" show that she has reached the second step. The child in underpants who never notices poop or wetness is not ready; put the diapers back on for a few months. (A few children are much less sensitive to their own body sensations than the majority. They are less likely to notice their need to use the potty until the last moment. In this case, routines and timing can be more important than the child's age.)

The realization of "is going" is important, but it's the last step that indicates a child is close to being trained: the knowledge of "needing to go." When your daughter comes to you and says, "Dad, I need to pee," get up and put her on the toilet immedi-

The need to go

ately. She has made a connection between her mind and body; she can hold the urine in until she is on the toilet and then release it.

Watch for the time when your child knows where things like

shoes, coats, purses, grocery bags, and dirty laundry belong. Since she now knows that certain items belong in special places, she'll also understand better that pee and poop go in the toilet.

Key Steps in Intellectual Readiness
- Uses toileting words
- Aware that he "has gone"
- Aware that he "is going"
- Aware that he "needs to go"

EMOTIONAL READINESS

Inborn temperament traits affect emotional readiness. Curious, adaptable children often look for, take on, and enjoy new challenges. If your child has a very regular body and thus poops at the same time each day, it will be easier to make that potty stop a part of your basic, daily routine. Adaptability and regularity are traits that make toilet training a little easier.

Change is much harder for some temperament types than for others. It's a myth that all children want to give up wet and messy diapers. Wearing diapers is all they've known since birth and it feels normal. Peeing and pooping in the toilet can be scary—especially for more cautious children. Some children fear they'll fall in and be flushed away. Other children don't like their poop (part of their bodies) falling out of them and disappearing into the toilet.[2]

If children appear fearful and reluctant, pushing them to perform does no good. If your son states clearly, "No, I don't like the toilet," no amount of coaxing and persuading is going to change his mind. To become emotionally ready, a child needs acceptance of his fears and reassurance that Mom and Dad respect the fact that it's his body and ultimate control lies with him.

Do not engage in a power struggle. It's best to back off and try another approach later. Emotional power struggles—a battle of wills between parent and child—over toileting are counter-productive to training (more on this in Chapter 6).

Guiding your child to use the toilet usually takes place between the

---

[2] The book *Toilet Learning* by Alison Mack includes a section for children about where their poop and pee go when flushed. See the Resource section at the end of this book.

ages of two and three, when a child is pushing hard to be independent. This adds to the challenge of training. Children become independent by defining themselves as separate from you. Non-compliance and negativity are normal and important parts of this developmental stage. Statements such as, "No! Me do it!" and "Leave me alone!" usually peak around two and a half. (Though, like all developmental milestones, some children reach this point sooner, and others, later.)

It seems unfortunate that physical and intellectual readiness for potty training often come together just when rebellion is on the rise! However, believe it or not, there is a benefit to toilet training and the "Terrible Two's" going hand in hand. Children control their attitudes and emotional responses to any situation. They alone control what their bodies do. Ultimately, it is the child who decides to be trained—*he* is in control of his body. Instructing your children to use the toilet really shows you where your influence begins and ends. As a parent, there's a lot you can do to influence your child's behavior, but your control only extends so far. You have to learn how to positively direct your child toward the desired goal, all the while respecting her as a separate individual with her own unique temperament and style of learning. This is a valuable parenting skill to acquire.

Work with—not against—your two year old. This is easy advice to give, but often difficult to carry out. Your goal is to skillfully convince your two year old that using the toilet is her idea. Use positive influence and resist pressure tactics. If you sense yourself getting exasperated, tense, or angry, back off. Readjust your frame of mind. Don't engage in a power struggle; you'll lose. Pressure won't work. Respect from you for this separateness contributes to children's self-esteem and personal responsibility.

Social, intellectual, and physical readiness are all often easier to detect than emotional readiness. So back off and try again in a couple of months. A child who is emotionally ready is eager and interested to try to use the toilet.

Ultimately, emotional readiness means day-in, day-out willingness to respond promptly to bodily needs. Don't let one success lure you into believing your child is now completely trained. You'll hear parents claim their child was trained in one day. This may be true for a few children, but most learn to use the toilet gradually over about one month's time. Peeing or pooping in the toilet occasionally can be interesting and fun. Expect back sliding. Paying attention all day, every day, requires much more emotional maturity. Build on your child's successes, but don't believe that one poop in the toilet will lead to complete training. Rather, recognize each successful step as part of the process.

Some children sneak off to their bedroom to poop in their diapers. This tells parents the child is ready intellectually because she understands the "need to go," but may not be ready to give up her diapers. She lacks emotional readiness. It's okay; all she needs is time and reassurance that she's the one in control. Say, "You can wait until you feel ready to poop in the potty." If there is no change in several months, encourage a step in the right direction. You could say, "The bathroom is the place for poops. When you need to poop, you can go to the bathroom, close the door, and poop in your diaper there."[3]

Treating your child's body with dignity supports emotional readiness. Treat his or her body respectfully, whether you're assisting with wiping, or simply honoring your child's request for privacy.

Stories from the Bathroom

Fear of Falling In *(Ryan, almost 3)*

A week before Ryan's third birthday, he was reluctant and unwilling to potty train. He didn't like that little potty chair on the floor and he wouldn't sit on the plastic ring that fit on the big toilet either. It wobbled.

Ryan was ready physically, intellectually, and socially, but emotionally he wasn't quite there. Finally, one day he agreed to sit on the big toilet, but he wanted to do it without the plastic ring.

Mom and Dad were encouraged. So Ryan sat on the toilet, teetering back and forth, trying to get his

—continued on next page

---

[3] (See the anecdote *No Diaper, No Poop* in Chapter 6, page 91.)

—continued from previous page

balance. Then, he slipped. His little bottom dropped into the toilet. Not only did the fall frighten him, he was also terrified of being flushed away. He yelled, "Don't flush the toilet! Don't flush the toilet!"

Mom pulled him out, held him, and affirmed how scary it was for him. After that, of course, Ryan was more determined than ever not to use the toilet. Days passed. Mom kept asking him if he'd like to try. All she got were flat-out refusals.

Finally Dad took the initiative. He said, "Come on, Ryan, let's try again. I'll hold you on the toilet so you won't fall." Ryan resisted, but Dad confidently set him on the toilet anyway. Dad crouched around the toilet, encircling Ryan with his arms. Dad reassured him, "I'm here. I won't let you fall in. You're safe. Go ahead; you can pee in the toilet just like Dad." Ryan didn't pee, but his fears began to disappear. Each evening Dad included taking him to the toilet as part of the bedtime routine. After three days of following this routine, Ryan finally did urinate in the toilet.

Dad knew Ryan needed emotional support to help him on the road to toilet training. All it took was some reassurance and understanding. Dad also sensed the hard-line approach—"Get in there right now and pee in that toilet. How can you be afraid of a dumb old toilet? What are you, a baby?"—would probably result in power struggles and frustration for all.

This was the beginning for Ryan. He was getting over his fear of the toilet and emotionally he was on his way to being trained. For a week or so, Mom and Dad held him safely in place as he peed and pooped. Finally, Ryan felt confident enough to balance alone on the toilet without assistance. In less than three weeks, he was totally trained.

THE TEMPERAMENT FACTOR

In addition to readiness, your child's inborn temperament also affects the training process. Here are basic traits and tips to keep in mind as you look ahead to toilet training.

Trait	Effects on Toilet Training and Strategies
Regularity— of body rhythms	**Regular** bio-rhythms make potty training easier because you can generally predict when poops are likely. With **irregular** bio-rhythms, bowel movements come at different times each day—pay more attention to body signals than to the time of day.
Sensitivity— awareness of body sensations	**Highly sensitive** children more easily notice the internal signals from bladder and bowels and may dislike the feel of wet or messy diapers. On the other hand, they may also be upset by the noise of flushing or when they have accidents (pee or poop where it doesn't belong). A fluffy, inviting toilet seat cover may be better than a cold, hard toilet seat and thus gain more cooperation. **Less sensitive** children are rarely bothered by wet or messy diapers and don't easily notice the need to use the toilet. They may train later than others. Invite them to put a hand on their tummy to see if they can notice the feelings inside.
Intensity— dramatic or mellow	**High intensity** children have strong feelings about everything—including the potty. Listen to their concerns. They will get upset if you are upset, so pretend calm if you need to. Help them see a personal benefit in using the toilet.
Cautious or Curious— first reaction to new things	**Cautious** children need a slow introduction to bathroom equipment—well before they are expected to use it. Watch **curious** children closely as they may want to experiment and put lots of things *down* the toilet. Let them flush after you, or flush down a drop of food coloring.

—continued on next page

—continued from previous page

Trait	Effects on Toilet Training and Strategies
Adaptability— ability to handle transitions	**Highly adaptable** children usually adjust easily to daily changes—including getting to the toilet. **Less adaptable** children (better called "natural planners") do better when they know what is ahead—when they have a plan for what is coming. Talk *ahead of time* about upcoming toilet training. Leaving an activity to go to the toilet is hard, so make a plan, such as, "I will take my truck with me when I have to go to the bathroom."
Energy level	**High energy** kids may need to wiggle their toes, clap their hands, talk, or sing in order to stay on the potty for a few minutes.
Distractibility	**Highly distractible** children are likely to need your help to stay seated on the potty long enough to relax and poop. Be ready to sit and talk with them, read, or bring along some toys.
Frustration Reaction	**Easily frustrated** children get discouraged if success isn't immediate. Plan small steps toward potty independence so they see success along the way.

READINESS CHECKLIST

The chart below lists signs of toilet training readiness. If your child is not yet ready, there are important things you can begin doing now (or as early as 18 months) to lay the groundwork for training (see Chapter 3). With relaxed preparation ahead of time, both you and your child will be ready when the time comes.

Physical Readiness
☐ Diaper is dry at least an hour and a half at a time.
☐ Child has already mastered walking and running so has energy for new learning.
☐ Child enjoys sitting in one place for a few minutes and playing with toys.

Social Readiness
☐ Shows interest in toileting. Follows you and others into the bath-

room to watch you on the toilet. Likes being part of the bathroom social scene.

☐ Plays at toileting. Puts dolls or stuffed animals on the toilet and pretends they're going potty.

Intellectual Readiness

☐ Imitates your behavior—cooking, shaving, shopping.

☐ Understands place—likes to put shoes, coats, and books where they belong.

☐ Shows awareness of elimination:

> * *Knows when she "has gone."* Indicates that her diapers are wet or full, or that she has just peed or pooped.
> * *Knows when she "is going."* Recognizes when she is in the process of peeing or pooping. (For example, the child may stop playing when she's pushing a poop into her diaper.)
> * *Knows when she "needs to go."* Indicates that she needs to use the potty.

Emotional Readiness

☐ Is comfortable with, rather than afraid of, the toilet, or of sitting on the potty.

☐ Is willing to sit briefly on the toilet.

If you checked off most of the above, your child is ready for toileting instruction.

POTTY TRAINING AVERAGES

Although every child proceeds on his or her own timetable, it can be helpful to look at statistics of average times children achieve potty training milestones. Today, 50% of girls train by two and a half and 50% of boys train by age three.

The data in the chart below was collected by the author in a study of approximately 100 children. The ages shown are the average times boys and girls from this group reached each milestone. (For children who experienced regression, it occurred between the ages of 31 to 35 months. The regression lasted, on average, about one month.)

Children's Toilet Training Progress by Months[4]

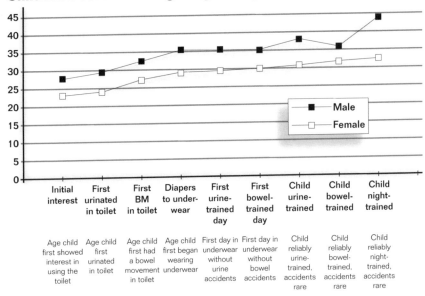

Initial interest	First urinated in toilet	First BM in toilet	Diapers to under-wear	First urine-trained day	First bowel-trained day	Child urine-trained	Child bowel-trained	Child night-trained
Age child first showed interest in using the toilet	Age child first urinated in toilet	Age child first had a bowel movement in toilet	Age child first began wearing underwear	First day in underwear without urine accidents	First day in underwear without bowel accidents	Child reliably urine-trained, accidents rare	Child reliably bowel-trained, accidents rare	Child reliably night-trained, accidents rare

---

[4] Data from a study of Washington state families, conducted by Jan Faull, 1995.

2

The Parent's Role in Potty Training

Toilet training with ease is the hope of all parents. Before looking further at your child, it's helpful to consider your role. One mom asked this question, "What if you did nothing when it comes to toilet training? Would your child eventually learn to pee and poop in the toilet on his own?"

It's just about impossible for a parent to do nothing. Simply because parents use the toilet themselves, children get the message they are expected to eventually learn to use the toilet too. Some children ease into training with little more than a few suggestions from Mom or Dad and some practice. When their bowel and bladder muscles develop and strengthen, they learn to use the toilet without much effort. For most children, however, training is a process. You model the desired behavior and serve as your child's mentor. You offer guidance, positive attention, and interest.

Picture a basketball game. Your child is the player. Most of the time the parent's role is that of cheerleader. As a member of the cheering squad, you're thrilled and enthusiastic with each step he takes toward victory. If your child has a few accidents or even regresses temporarily, you don't get discouraged. You know that, sooner or later, success will happen. Even if he appears to be down by twenty points in the potty training game, any slight advancement gets applause. As toileting cheerleader, you don't necessarily need pom poms and a "sis boom bah." What your child needs from you is simply positive attention for any interest he shows or slight advances he makes in toileting skills.

Sometimes a parent's role is that of coach. There are times when you need to step in, teach some skills, develop a few rules, or provide some clear discipline as you guide your child toward using the toilet. All good coaches recognize the importance of practice, practice, practice. The parent-as-coach needs to sense when the time is right to nudge the player into learning the next skill and gaining more competence. There are also times when a parent needs to referee; it's up to you to establish some rules and guidelines for potty training.

Most of the time, however, you are a cheerleader. Just as a cheering squad never gets down on the team, you never get down on your child. When ultimate success occurs, you're relieved and thrilled. A developmental milestone has been reached. However, it's important to remember that it is the child's achievement and victory, not yours.

PARENTING STYLES

Each parent has an approach to parenting that is evident in how they train their child to do anything—from sleeping through the night, to toilet training, to helping children complete their homework. Your general approach toward parenting will certainly impact how you approach toilet training. Your parenting style may also suggest which way you need to move in order to become the cheerleader your child needs for successful potty training. There are three distinct parenting styles. Notice the category where you fit.

The Take-Charge Parent

These parents have a take-charge approach. They supervise children closely and are strict and clear about their expectations. When they think the right time has come, they are decisive and teach the child to use the toilet. They don't hedge. They develop a plan and proceed with confidence.

Children are accustomed to using diapers. The parent's job is to cultivate an interest in using the toilet. Take-Charge parents need to be careful that toileting doesn't become more important to them than it is to the child. Attention, guidance, and support are needed to make this transition from diapers to underpants.

The Diplomatic Parent

These parents have goals when it comes to guiding their children, but are quick to adapt their expectations according to the child's individual development and temperament. They follow signs of the child's readiness whether they are teaching the child to use the toilet or ride a bicycle. They observe their children's progress and respond accordingly.

These parents show enthusiasm, but don't apply pressure. They incorporate a low level of determination without being too relaxed. They know that guiding a child to use the toilet doesn't always miraculously occur.

The Laissez-Faire Parent

The laissez-faire approach is the third style. Parents in this category are less intrusive when it comes to guiding their children. They don't make too many demands. They trust that, in time, children—mostly on their own—will learn manners, tidiness, and toileting. Discipline is low key and unimposing.

Many parents who take this laid-back approach are uninvolved or overly busy with other things. Others are very involved, but believe a gentle, accepting, and non-intrusive style fosters a loved and accomplished child. With today's child-centered approach to toilet training, sometimes these parents relax too much and wait for the child to train himself. They don't nudge their child, even a little, because they fear it will leave psychological scars.

There are other reasons parents might fail to initiate training. Some parents don't encourage their child to use the toilet even when the child displays most of the readiness signs. Their lives are stressful enough without adding potty training; the convenience of diapers makes it easy to let toilet training wait. Other parents fail to take time to adequately orient their child to the toileting process. The result is a delay of training and some children even become resistant to the toileting process altogether.

Which category do you fall into? When it comes to toilet training, each discipline style will work with some children and not with others. However, parents who embrace the diplomatic style are usually most successful when it comes to toilet training. The take-charge parent, for example, might need to back off. A parent with a laissez-faire style might need to become more actively involved with toilet training. And even the diplomatic parent can go awry; this parent can come across as wishy-washy to the child. The diplomatic parent sometimes tries too hard to be in tune with the child and changes her approach to toilet training frequently, hoping to find the method best suited to the child, but just ends up confusing the child. The following stories show possible pitfalls with the different approaches.

Stories from the Bathroom

A Take-Charge Parent Uses Too Much Pressure
(Vincent, 2½ years)

David wanted his son to be trained. He was clear and determined. He put Vincent in underpants and told him to keep his pants dry and clean. He made it clear that Vincent was expected to pee and poop in the toilet.

Vincent balked. He had accident after accident and refused to perform on the toilet. He wet or pooped his pants right after sitting on the toilet seat. After a week of no success, David realized that he must alter his tactics. He put Vincent back in diapers. He set him on the toilet twice a day to practice and then started using underpants part-time until his son gained control. Slowly, Vincent became willing to use the toilet.

Vincent made it perfectly clear he needed a more gradual approach when it came to learning to use the toilet. He just couldn't succeed with his dad's first method. Even though it wasn't David's natural parenting style to back off, he managed to do it. He didn't give up; he simply provided a more flexible, alternate plan. In this way, David helped Vincent gradually take charge of his own bodily functions.

—continued on next page

—continued from previous page

Waiting Longer than Necessary *(Mike, 3½ years)*

Kathy was confused; she knew not to push her child to use the toilet, so ended up doing nothing in fear of doing something wrong. She waited and hoped Mike would just train himself. The toilet became a novelty item he avoided. The result: Mike side-stepped the toilet and training until well into his third year, beyond what was necessary.

Mike was Kathy's first child so she was understandably unsure about how to approach training. Finally, she mustered up the courage, hid her anxieties, adopted a confident attitude, and set aside time each day for underpants, accidents, and toileting instruction. It was a few short days before Mike was in underpants full-time.

COMBINING DIFFERENT PARENTING STYLES TO SOLVE PROBLEMS

Knowing your parenting style can help you discern how best to solve potty training problems. See how these parents identified their own trouble spots and changed tactics.

Stories from the Bathroom

Diplomatic Mom Sets a Limit *(Daniel, 2½ years)*

Marie asked Daniel each day if he wanted to wear diapers or underwear. She wanted Daniel to choose; she believed that he needed to be in charge. But the daily decision to wear diapers or underpants went on way too long. About three days a week, Daniel chose diapers; on the other days, he chose underpants.

—continued on next page

—continued from previous page

Finally, it appeared that Daniel had control of his bowels and bladder, but on the days he wore diapers, he didn't bother with using the toilet. The daily routine of choosing underpants or diapers was hindering complete toilet training success. Marie hated to do it, but finally she declared, "No more diapers."

Daniel pouted, complained, and cried, but Mom remained firm in her stand. She was uncomfortable with Daniel's emotional response and wanted to spare him discomfort, but both she and Daniel endured the tears. In three days, Daniel gave up asking for diapers and used the toilet consistently.

A Low Key Mom Imposes Some Structure
(Tameeka, 3 years)

LaTonya was low key in her approach to parenting—including toilet training. Then this scenario began to occur: her daughter had an accident almost every time they went for a ride in the car. LaTonya hoped Tameeka would learn on her own to pee before getting in the car, but her daughter continued to have accident after accident. Finally, LaTonya lost her patience.

Although it was contrary to her parenting style, LaTonya imposed a rule: Tameeka must try to pee in the toilet before any car ride. Of course, LaTonya couldn't force Tameeka to perform on the toilet, but most often Tameeka would go. LaTonya needed to change her laid-back approach so her daughter could be spared the embarrassment and hassle of wet clothes on every outing in the car.

When more than one person is involved in guiding a child to use the toilet, conflict can arise. If one adult is more easygoing, while another is more determined to get the task accomplished, they may argue or proceed with two completely different methods. The child becomes unnecessarily confused and frustrated. Whose rules should he follow? On the other hand, when parents provide consistency, children learn more quickly and easily. If conflict develops between parents or caregivers, it needs to be resolved before you can proceed with training. Parents need to find the middle ground—compromise, negotiate, and develop one plan for toilet training their child. Here's how one diplomatic mom and take-charge dad met in the middle for their child's sake.

Stories from the Bathroom

Parents Learn to Work Together *(Logan, 3 years)*

Alexis started teaching Logan to use the toilet in her usual diplomatic manner. When Dad came home, he took on the task with more force and determination. He set rules: no more diapers; any accidents and TV privileges were taken away. Logan was confused by the difference in styles and did not make much progress. Finally, the couple sought counseling.

This is how they resolved the conflict. Because Alexis was the primary caregiver, she would be in charge of teaching Logan to use the toilet. But when Dad came home, he and Logan would use the toilet together, including a practice time on the toilet before bedtime. Dad was able to provide some rules and be Logan's positive role model without confusing Logan about whose approach to follow. Dad's new plan for the evening fit in with Mom's more relaxed approach during the day. Logan benefited from Dad's involvement and the new consistency of style. He soon made progress.

TACTICS FOR SUCCESSFUL TRAINING

Here are some steps to ease your path through the training process—setting aside time, dealing with setbacks and criticism, as well as maintaining a good relationship with your child. Planning ahead will help things go more smoothly.

Find Time

An important ingredient required for training is time. Be prepared to set aside some of your regular activities because you'll need extra energy to take on potty training. Teaching your child to use the toilet requires you to carefully and quietly monitor your child's progress.

Stories from the Bathroom

Storm-bound *(Jenna, 2 years)*

Anna was a busy mom. She had a two year old and a new baby, plus worked part-time, volunteered for community projects, managed her home, shopped, exercised, and entertained. One Seattle winter it snowed for a week. Anna was housebound, so her life was forced to slow down. That week she trained her daughter, Jenna.

Two years later, a windstorm hit Seattle; parts of the city were shut down without power for five long days. Again, Anna was housebound. That week she trained her two-year-old son.

Stay Calm during Setbacks

Toilet training proceeds easily for many parents and children. Some children, however, resist the whole process. This is very stressful for whatever parenting style is in play. Remember this: toilet training is important, but it's *more* important that your child develops positive associations with the toileting process. If you yell, spank, coerce, or manipulate your child to use the toilet, he may grow to resist and resent one of the most common and natural functions in daily life. Your positive and pleasant demeanor is so important.

Cope with Criticism from Others

Parents today must prepare themselves for an avalanche of unsolicited advice from friends, neighbors, and family members. Anyone who ever trained a child has advice and opinions. Remember, the age at which your child uses the toilet doesn't determine your skill as a parent. Additionally, there is little connection between the age of toilet training and a child's IQ.

Toilet training can be a frustrating and emotionally charged process.

Parents need the support of others, not their criticism. When you approach toileting instruction differently from others, they might conclude you think the way they trained their children is wrong. Be sensitive to this and don't argue. When someone gives their opinion, listen, nod, thank them for their advice, and then train your child the way you think is best. There's no need to get defensive; a battle with others about toilet training is a waste of time and energy.

Here's all you need to say to anyone who offers unsolicited advice, "There certainly are different approaches to toilet training. It's interesting to hear how you accomplished the task. I appreciate your ideas."

You know your child better than anyone. Be confident that your careful thought and planning will serve your child well and get on with training.

Maintain a Loving Relationship

A positive, patient attitude about toilet training is essential. The better your overall relationship is with your child, the more influence you will have in your child's life and the easier it will be to teach him new skills. Never take it for granted that your child knows how much you love him. You must demonstrate it with your words and actions every day. Here are some suggestions.

- Observe your child. As your son puts his doll on and off the toilet in play, stop to observe. When your daughter is drawing a picture, ask if you can watch. As she practices the piano, sit down and listen. This sounds simple, but it's an easy and powerful way to express a silent, "I love you."

- Participate in your child's interests and hobbies. When he takes an interest in the toilet, support that interest. Let him flush the toilet for you or give you toilet paper. When your children are older, go to their dance recitals, school performances, and soccer games. Hunt through baseball card shops for that special, sought-after card. Children's interests are important. When you support their interests, you're telling them they are important to you. Showing interest strengthens the parent-child relationship.

- Seek opportunities daily to communicate love through gentle touch. When your child tries to poop into the toilet, kneel down and gently touch her back or legs. Pull him on your lap to read a story. Cuddle her when she's sad. Massage his back, legs, and arms when his muscles are tired from a long day at play. Touch communicates love without saying a word.

- Tell your child you love him. Do it routinely as you tuck him in bed each night, or spontaneously as you're changing his diaper, or as he sits on the potty chair for the first time. As your child works on a puzzle, or when he's older and doing his homework, bestow an "I love you." When your child sits on your lap, whisper, "I'm glad you're my kid." It will feel good to your child—and to you too.

- Complete cycles of conversation. When your toddler says, "My teddy pooped his pants," don't ignore him. Instead, respond, "You better change him. I bet he'll learn to poop in the toilet someday." When your eight year old says, "My friend Chloe is moving to Chicago," don't just say, "Oh" or "Don't worry, you'll find another friend." Instead respond this way, "When is she moving?" and "I'll bet you'll miss her." Your reply communicates, "I heard what you said, I'm interested, and I want to hear more."

- Guide your child clearly and respectfully toward appropriate behavior. There are ways to discipline that preserve dignity and self-esteem and there are attempts at discipline that tear down a child's self-image. Some days you'll get it right, some days you won't.

   Upholding a rule provides security in a child's world; this equals love. Insisting a child sit on the toilet to try to pee before a car ride provides a reasonable limit, develops a positive routine, and brings security and predictability to a child's life. Reasonable rules, even though they may elicit a little emotional resistance from the child as they're being taught, are a powerful expression of love. Rules tell your child you care.

- Help them out. If Benjamin is struggling to get his pants up after peeing in the toilet, leave your phone conversation to help him. If Lily is struggling to find her backpack, lunch box, or coat as she's running out the door for the school bus, help her out. If your children want to build a fort, but are frustrated gathering the materials and developing the plans, step in and help. Don't take over and don't do it for them—just help.

- Compliment your child. Notice baby steps toward competency. "I saw you sitting on the toilet trying to pee—good for you." "I saw you take your plate from the table to the counter—I really appreciate that." "I was so proud of you today when you thanked Grandma for the cookies. Such nice manners." These compliments not only reinforce positive behavior, but because you took time to notice, they also say, "I love you."
- Cheer your child on. As your child begins to use the toilet, quietly cheer each success. Any effort toward competency deserves your applause. Whether it's reading, basketball, or working on a model airplane, offer encouragement. And when she experiences failure, be there to wipe her tears. Help her learn from her mistakes and try another approach.
- Brag to others about your child when she can overhear. Call Dad at work with the news, "Ryder sat on the toilet and peed twice today." If someone else compliments your child, repeat it to your child. Some parents worry (in an old-fashioned sense) that praise will produce conceited children. Certainly we don't want little princes and princesses running around believing every little thing they do is just darling, but we do want children who are quietly self-assured. So go ahead and do some bragging and let your child hear it.

All parents love their children, but it takes skill to demonstrate this love. When you and your child are connected by a relationship based in love, it will be easier for you to teach your child to use the toilet and many other necessary skills.

3

Places to Start

There is no one perfectly prescribed plan for guiding your child to use the toilet. Some children literally train themselves, not wanting any assistance or coaching. Others are reluctant and ignore any potty training efforts, then seem to miraculously train in their own way and time. Most ease into using the toilet with guidance, encouragement, and a flexible plan initiated by parents and child care providers.

LAYING THE GROUNDWORK

Even before your child is physically, intellectually, socially, and emotionally ready, there's much you can do to prepare for success. Taking steps ahead of time helps ensure that your child's window of opportunity for training won't slip by.

Around 10 Months, Start Using Toileting Words

As you routinely change diapers, start using your preferred bathroom words: clean, dry, wet, poopy, or whatever you deem best for your family. Regularly use the words "sit" and "go." If your child resists diaper changes, plant the following thought in her mind: "When you pee and poop in the potty, you won't have to wear diapers."

Around 18 Months Start the Following...

- Take your child with you when you use the toilet (if you don't already do so). Copying others is an important way that children learn.
- Talk about what you're doing when you are in the bathroom.

- Let the child flush when you're done.
- Buy a potty chair for the bathroom so if she wants to copy you and sit nearby, she can do so.
- Focus attention on your child whenever she or he shows interest in the toilet.
- Include a book about using the potty among your regular bedtime stories. Choose a book appropriate to your child's age and gender. (See the list of children's books in the Resource section at the end of this book.) Check your local library or bookstore.
- Talk about all who use the potty: grandparents, neighbors, characters in books.
- Point out when neighborhood dogs, cats, and birds do their business outside. Tell your child that people do this in the potty!

Then When the Time Feels Right...

Most American families currently start potty training between 23 to 31 months of age. Children become independent toilet users, on average, between two and a half to four years old. By age four, 90% have reached this major milestone. Training usually takes about six months, though some children get it in a few days and others need 12 months. This brings up the question: Is your child likely to train earlier or later than age mates?

Temperament factors that make early training more likely include:
- High awareness of body signals (thirsty, tired, feeling pain, etc.)
- Able to quickly adapt during transitions (leaving the house, getting to the table for a meal, going to bed at night, etc.)
- Having low or moderate energy (so sitting is easy).
- Being generally mellow and cooperative in mood.

Temperament factors which make later training more likely are pretty much the opposite end of the spectrum for the qualities detailed above:
- Low awareness of body signals.
- Needing lots of time to adjust to new things or changes in schedule.
- Having high energy levels (sitting still is hard).
- Difficulty with routine transitions and unexpected changes (running to the toilet requires a change of plans!)

If you know your child is likely to train later, the earlier you begin, the longer the process will take.

Some children announce they are ready, while others wait for adults to take the lead. If your child hasn't initiated the process by three years, it's time to step in and show the way. Here are steps you can take when you feel the time is right:

- Move the potty chair to the main living area of the house. Move it around from room to room with you, or, if you live in a large or split-level home, you may want to have several potty chairs. This way, your child has more opportunity to become familiar with the potty chair and it is close when needed. It becomes a part of daily living rather than just something off in the bathroom.
- Continue to take your child with you when you go to use the toilet.
- Encourage your child to put dolls and teddy bears on the toilet. Your child will come to understand this potty business through play.
- If your child is three or older, and especially if he or she doesn't see other children using the potty, consider watching a DVD about toilet training together. (See the Resource section.)

Practice with Diapers On

Whether or not you need this step (and the following one) depends on your child's temperament. Some children have a natural interest in new things. They quickly adjust to and accept changes in daily living. They initiate and rehearse new things on their own. For them, practice before potty training is not necessary. For other children, practice potty-sitting with diapers on is an important step toward helping them feel comfortable and emotionally ready to move forward. Whether you start this practice at 18 months or later, depends on your child's individual development and temperament. Realistically, you want to start practice sessions either before or after the "No!" stage of resistance that commonly occurs around age two and a half. Some emotionally intense children begin this "No!" stage early, around 14 to 18 months, while mellow children rarely resist until age three and a half.

For children who need time to make transitions, let the toileting process begin with practice, not performance. You can compare it to eating. Think about how strange it would be to your child if you nursed or bottle-fed him until he was two and a half and then suddenly you set him in the high chair and expected him to eat solid food three times a day with a fork and spoon. The child would be baffled and resistant. Of course, parents don't do this. We gradually introduce solid foods and independent eating and eventually wean children from the breast and the bottle. Many of the meals in the high chair end up being only practice sessions because children often play with the food and eat very little. The same approach applies to toilet training. Parents gradually introduce the potty chair and eventually eliminate diapers. Children need lots of opportunities for rehearsing the toileting procedure along the way.

Start inviting your child to sit briefly on his potty seat twice a day. If your child has shown little interest in toileting, you might need to impose a routine to establish the habit of these practice sessions. Don't take his diaper off at first. The child can remain fully clothed. Some however, will *want* their clothes and diaper off. This is not about actually using the potty, so don't expect performance. You're just getting your child familiar with the process. Do this at two regular times—perhaps before getting dressed or before bath time. The potty needs to be part of his daily routine. Some parents choose a time before lunch, before bath time, after dinner, or before bedtime—you can choose whatever time works best for your child.

Don't *ask* your child if he wants to sit on the toilet—just take him. He could very well answer, "No." Instead, use a firm, friendly, and clear approach, "Oh remember, we have a new rule: We *always* sit on the toilet before getting dressed." Even if your child is a little reluctant, don't hesitate; proceed with confidence.

Offer a choice if necessary, "Do you want to look at a book or hold your teddy while you sit on the potty chair?" Let your toddler take whatever he wants with him to the toilet. Toddlers love to tote toys around the house. The trip to the bathroom goes easier if your toddler takes a favorite toy along for company. The psychology works this way: You get your child to sit on the potty and your child gets to choose a toy or book for company. Both of you get something out of the visit to the bathroom.

Be persistent and consistent—not forceful, just firm and kind. Use an inviting tone of voice, "Oh yes, remember, we *always* sit on the toilet after breakfast." Children often respond well when you nickname these sessions something like, "Poo-Poo Time." If your child won't sit at first, set a doll on the toilet and talk about how the doll is peeing in the toilet. You can also offer a book to look at.

Age two is generally a good time to include potty visits in the daily routine. Most two year olds love regular, predictable routines, so if you forget, your child may soon be reminding you. Including practice sessions in her daily schedule helps your child make the transition from using diapers to using the toilet. With this approach, chances are better that when your child is physically ready, she will be emotionally ready as well, because sitting on the toilet will already be familiar.

It's essential to be clear about the importance of these visits to the toilet. Use a purposeful voice as you walk your child to the bathroom. Then once your child is on the toilet or potty chair, make it a pleasant time for you and your child to be together. Surround your child with love and nurture. Sing songs. Tell stories. Be at your parenting best here. You want your child to have pleasant associations with toileting.

Think of the interest, love, patience, and guidance you focused on your child when she learned to walk. That's the same interest and support your child needs as she learns to use the toilet. Notice and describe each minor success along the way. "Good for you. You're grunting and trying to push out a poop." Jumping up and down with praise is less important than carefully describing each minor success and focusing on your child with approving expressions as she sits on the toilet.

Stories from the Bathroom

Story Time (LeShawn, 2 years)

Kaneesha put a basket of little books in the bathroom. She'd entice LeShawn by saying, "It's Poo-Poo Time. You can choose one book for me to read to you while you sit there." Sometimes she would encourage LeShawn to carry a toy with him to the bathroom, asking, "It's time to sit on the potty again—would you like to take your truck with you?"

—continued on next page

—continued from previous page

Sitting Daily *(Chandra, 2½ years)*

Tricia wanted to start Chandra on the road to toileting. She'd ask Chandra, "Do you want to sit on the potty?"Chandra's consistent reply was, "No."But then Tricia realized Chandra was saying "No" to almost everything—ice cream, play school, going to the park—all things she really enjoyed. So Tricia stopped asking and just started taking her to the bathroom. At first she would kick and scream as her mother confidently carried her to the bathroom. Tricia would sit Chandra on the toilet, lovingly hold her there and say encouragingly, "Someday you'll pee and poop in the toilet." Soon Chandra was automatically sitting on the toilet each morning before climbing into the bathtub.

The mother in the above story realized her daughter wasn't specifically resisting toilet training, she was resisting the change being imposed on her life. This child adjusted to the practice sessions after three short days. If, after a week, your child continues to resist, you might consider waiting a bit and re-introducing the potty-sitting time again in a month.

Practice with Diapers Off

After your child has the routine of sitting on the potty at least twice a day, remove the diapers for the potty-sitting time. Don't expect any success as yet, but speak in encouraging terms, "Someday you'll pee and poop in the potty just like Mom, Dad, and sister. Right now you're just practicing."

Don't be surprised if your child protests. Since you're probably steering your child to use the toilet somewhere between the ages of two and three years old, a child at this age may protest *any* rules you impose. This is normal behavior, especially at two and a half. It's a fine line parents walk here; you want to be firm and kind, but not harsh or forceful. Remember, your child will feel competent and grown-up when she can pee and poop into the toilet. You're just helping the process along.

Accept your child's feelings and then proceed matter-of-factly. "I know you don't want to take your diapers off and sit on the toilet, but remember, we *always* sit on the toilet before leaving the house and now we must practice with your diapers off."If your child only sits there for two seconds, praise her. "Good for you, you sat on the toilet." Don't plead for more cooperation; don't shrug your shoulders and act defeated. She sat there for two seconds—next time she'll probably sit longer. If there are any accidental successes, be enthusiastic.

BEFORE STARTING ACTUAL TRAINING

Change your child frequently and say, "I'm changing your diaper because it's wet (or messy)." Say this as a point of information—never with a hint of disapproval. Your child will begin to differentiate between wet and dry, and messy and clean. You can also add, "When you are ready, you'll use the potty." Saying, "When you are big girl (or boy), you'll use the potty," works fine for many children. Others are ambivalent about getting big, especially, for example, if there is a baby in the house who is getting a lot of attention during diaper changes.

Feeling the Difference between Wet and Dry

Many of today's well-clad toddlers get little body sensation from urinating; their very efficient and absorbent diapers mask the feeling of "wet." When potty training, however, the child needs to know when he is peeing. There are many options to make the natural difference between wet and dry more obvious.

- **Diapers with more sensation.** Because disposable diapers are highly absorbent and the plastic cover keeps everything warm, today's children can pee without any sensation of wetness on their skin. Some parents therefore change to cloth diapers before toilet training, so children more readily notice the process of peeing. If you use highly absorbent, washable "pocket diapers," try putting the cotton pad next to the child's skin, so wetness is more obvious.

- **Disposable training pants.** Often referred to as "Pull-Ups," these disposables are easy for children to get up and down. However, they feel like disposable diapers once in place and quickly wick moisture away from the skin, so they offer little opportunity to learn about wetness from skin sensation. To counteract this effect during training, manufacturers have tried to make the wet sensation in these disposables more obvious. However, the subtle changes in color or temperature are likely to be lost on many youngsters.

Parents generally have strong opinions about the use of disposable diapers and disposable training pants. There are pros and cons to their use, as with anything else. The most obvious advantage to them is the ease of cleanup compared to cloth training pants. If you are very concerned about accidents, these close-fitting, padded alternatives may help you feel more secure.

- **Washable cloth training pants.** These thick cotton underpants make the process of peeing much more obvious than diapers and are easy for children to pull up and down. They are a convenient way to bridge the transition from diapers to thinner underpants. They absorb the urine and hold up the stool, so if your child has an accident, there's rarely a mess on the floor, especially if you use plastic pants over them.

- **Lightweight underwear.** Thin, cloth underwear gives immediate feedback if your child has an accident, so it's an appropriate choice as long as cleanup isn't a problem for you. Some children learn the difference between the sensations of wet and dry, and messy and clean, more easily with thin, cloth underwear than with heavily padded underpants.

- **Naked.** Some parents train their children in the summer and skip clothes entirely. This is easy with a linoleum floor and a yard full of grass. There's nothing like pee running down your leg for instant feedback! In cooperative climates, you can train outdoors during the daytime and use diapers or training pants when indoors. Children who have low body sensation are much more likely to notice pee running down their leg than dampness against a well-padded bottom.

    If you think your child would benefit from "instant feedback," but you're uncomfortable with a naked bottom running around, try the lightweight underwear option instead.

Remember, there is no one right or wrong way to teach your child the difference between wet and dry. Each child is unique in his or her body and temperament. One child will succeed perfectly well in disposable Pull-Ups while the next will do better with cotton underwear. Only you know your child well enough to make the call. Do so with confidence.

Dressing for Training

Take your child to buy either the lightweight underwear or the thick, cotton training pants. There are many cute ones on the market. Whether your child prefers superheroes, or ruffles and lace, it's important to involve him or her in picking out the new underwear.

Dress your child in clothes that are easy to unfasten. Avoid jeans with a zipper, belts, snaps, jumpsuits, or overalls. Make it easy on your child to get pants up and down quickly with as little assistance from you as possible. Some parents dress their children for training in sweat pants with no underwear on at all. This makes it easy to get pants down quickly. Girls in dresses have it easy because they can lift up their dresses and pull down their panties quickly. Some parents let children run around naked so they are not encumbered at all.

Potty Chair or Toilet Seat?

Your child may have some distinct ideas about which he'll use—a potty chair that is placed on the floor or a seat that fits on the rim of the big toilet. Some of these inserts have steps attached; if not, you'll need to set her on the seat until she is big enough to climb up there by herself, or purchase a step stool at the same time.

Bowel movements are easier if children have a place to put their feet. It's difficult to push the poop out when feet are dangling; a footstool can help here. It's more work to clean the removable pot in a potty chair each time the child uses it. This task, however, is only temporary, as children soon advance to the household toilet.

Stories from the Bathroom

Big Toilet Only! *(Max, age 3)*

Mom bought a potty chair that sits on the floor for her son, Max. Then Aunt Jaime brought over the variety that fits on the big toilet—the one she used with her own children. Max had a choice; he could use the potty rim on the big toilet or he could use the free-standing potty chair. Max liked neither. He was determined to use the big toilet just like Mom and his big brother. He would balance there for bowel movements and to urinate. He never fell into the toilet, much to his mother and brother's amazement.

Stand Up or Sit down?

Do boys stand up or sit down to urinate while training? Some boys want to stand up just like Dad and big brother. Others begin by sitting down and pushing their penises down into the toilet so the pee hits the toilet bowl, rather than the floor. You must show or demonstrate these positions to your son.

If boys start out by sitting to pee, it's easier to catch poops at the same time. You may ask Dad to demonstrate this method until your son is pooping easily in the toilet. Boys who begin by sitting soon copy others who stand to pee. Some learn from observing neighborhood pals or bigger boys at preschool or child care. Some boys sit facing the back of the toilet to start and then eventually stand. (If, from the beginning, you make it part of the routine to put the toilet seat back down and flush, the women in your son's life will be appreciative.) Some girls are very frustrated to find that they can't stand and pee as their brothers can.

Urine vs. Bowel Training

Some children bowel train first, others urine train first, and some learn to do both at the same time. It is not unusual if your child learns to do one before the other. Bowel and bladder muscles are not the same. They are in different locations and offer a different set of "need-to-go" sensations. So if you see your child is having success peeing in the toilet, don't push bowel training right away. Let her accomplish urine training first and then take on bowel training.

Emptying the bowels is physically more complex than emptying the bladder. Abdominal muscles tighten to help empty the intestines. At the same time, muscles around the anus have to relax. This combination can be difficult to master, especially if the child is tense or worried.

Watch the Liquids

If a child drinks lots of liquids, it might be harder to train that child to urinate in the toilet. It just makes sense that the less liquid a child ingests, the easier the bladder will be to control. Keep an eye on how much your child is drinking, but take care not to dehydrate him.

Adults and children should generally drink enough water so that urine is light (straw colored), rather than dark, concentrated, and strong-smelling. Concentrated urine can irritate the bladder and make accidents more likely. Significant dehydration can decrease energy level and the ability to concentrate.

If you want more specific amounts, dietician Mary Silva, at www.drspock.com, reports that children generally need about 1½ ounces of fluid per pound of weight. Thus, a 20-pound toddler needs about 30 ounces of liquid per day. This amount includes not only milk, water, and juice, but also foods with high water content, such as yogurt, fruits, and vegetables. Your child's liquid requirements increase, of course, with hot weather, fever, or lots of drooling.

GETTING STARTED

The magical moment for potty training to officially begin is different for each child. Trust your intuition. You've watched your child develop daily from birth. You are tuned in to your child's readiness to take on any new challenge. So trust yourself and observe your child. If you know the time is right, then begin.

Don't start because you're feeling pressure from friends and relatives. Begin because all the signs point to the fact that the time is right for your child. If you're not sure, re-read the Readiness Checklist at the end of Chapter 1.

As you coach your child toward using the toilet, gently and calmly put the process into words. Offer short observations and explanations each step of the way. "Look at your teddy; he's sitting on the toilet going potty." "You peed in the toilet, good for you." Simple explanations regarding what is happening right now and what will happen next help children go from emotional response to intellectual understanding. Don't try to convince your child that your plan is a good one and don't expect agreement.

From this point, parents generally proceed in one of three different ways. Choose whichever best suits your child and your family life. No matter which approach you choose, be prepared for accidents. Most parents get daytime training established first and then move on to night training.

Approach Number One: Part-time Potty Training

Once your child has acquired the habit of practicing on the toilet without diapers, simply put on underpants for several hours each day.

Alternatively, set aside any convenient two-hour period during each day for toileting education. During this time the child wears underpants. Take your child to the toilet after the first hour to encourage him to relax and "let the pee pee out." If the child stays dry and clean and performs on the toilet, gradually extend the time he wears underpants until he has them on all day long.

Stories from the Bathroom

Only at Home *(Chris, 3 years)*

This approach worked for Mike, a busy single dad who was encouraging Chris to use the toilet. Chris was in a variety of child care settings—sometimes with Mom, Grandma, or in a family child care. It was too complicated to coordinate with all of them, so Mike decided that when he and Chris were home together in the evening, he'd put Chris in underpants.

Chris resisted—he liked his diapers. After all, he'd worn them since infancy. When Mike tried to talk him into wearing his big-boy underwear, Chris stomped his foot and said "No way." Mike backed off until the next night.

Then he tried this tactic: "Chris, there's a new rule in this house—when Chris and Dad are home together, Chris wears underwear." Chris looked at his dad a little stunned, but complied. At first, he had a few accidents, but after three days, he seldom wet his pants and always pooped in the toilet.

After a week, Mike put Chris in underwear full-time. At each child care setting Mike informed the caregiver of Chris's new toileting skill. There were some accidents as each child care provider worked with him, but soon he was successful no matter where he was.

Approach Number Two: Child's Choice Method

Some parents give their child a choice. Each morning, they ask the child if she wants to wear diapers or underpants. This is a good technique to use if there's an emotional power struggle brewing between parent and child. Having some say in the matter helps the child feel more in control of the process. On days (or half-days) with underpants, note how many accidents occur and if they diminish. Eventually, when you sense the time is right, end the diaper-wearing option.

Stories from the Bathroom

Underpants Today? *(Catalina, age 2½ years)*

Esmeralda used this technique with Catalina. Every morning she would ask, "Do you want to wear underpants or diapers today?" Some days Catalina would choose diapers, other days, underpants. After a week Catalina wasn't having any accidents when she wore underpants. So when the disposable diapers ran out, Esmeralda just told her, "The diapers are all gone. I'm not buying more at the store." Catalina didn't protest; she was ready for underpants full-time.

Approach Number Three: Full-time Training

Many parents feel the child is ready, bite the bullet and put their child in underpants full-time. Warn the child several days to one week prior to the event and begin on the designated day. This takes a lot of time and attention from the parent, but works for many families. Be prepared for accidents, adopt a matter-of-fact demeanor, and watch to see if the child gradually catches on to using the toilet full-time.

Stories from the Bathroom

Monday's the Day *(Andy, almost 3 years)*

This was Angela's approach. Her son, Andy, had practiced peeing and pooping on the toilet; he liked to set his favorite teddy bear on the toilet and pre-

—continued on next page

—continued from previous page

tend about toileting; he frequently watched Dad in the bathroom; he was telling Mom regularly when he was wet or his diapers were full; and he was dry for long periods during the day. Mom had prepared him for the official beginning of training by saying, "You know, next Monday you won't be wearing diapers anymore. You'll be wearing underpants just like Dad." They marked the days off on the calendar.

So the day came. At first Andy protested, "No, I want my diapers."But Mom insisted, "Remember, I told you, today you're going to wear your dinosaur underwear." With an unhappy face, Andy put on his underwear. He had several accidents the first day, fewer the next, and in five days, his accidents dwindled to one or two a week. After a month, he was trained.

Today Is the Day *(Winona, 2½ years)*

Winona's habit was to pee in the toilet every evening before climbing into the bathtub. It was part of the evening routine. Her mom, Nikki, wanted Winona trained and felt she was developmentally ready. Grandma was visiting, so Nikki saw this as the perfect time; Grandma would be there for moral support and to care for Winona's younger brother while Nikki was training Winona or cleaning up accidents.

One morning Mom just said, "Today you're going to wear the princess underwear we bought at the store." She let Winona pick out the pair she liked best and put them on her. She had accidents all day long—at least seven. As the day went on, she'd start to pee, notice it and then run to the bathroom to finish in the potty chair. Nikki let her do this without asking if Winona had to go because she didn't want her to get dependent on others for reminders. Winona began making progress on her own.

The second day they went to the shopping center. Winona announced she had to go, but by the time they found a toilet, she was soaked. After Mom cleaned her up, she set her on the toilet for a minute anyway.

—continued on next page

—continued from previous page

Winona didn't like to be wet or messy, so that helped a lot. They did bowel and urine training at the same time. The first two days were a mess. They just dealt with it. Winona urine trained first. Then one day Mom found her busy putting her dolls on and off the potty chair having them grunt and pretend to poop. She'd wipe one and then put another on. The next day she pooped in the toilet for the first time and only had a couple of accidents after that point.

Nikki gave her rewards throughout the training: a sticker for peeing in the toilet and an M&M® for pooping. If Nikki got frustrated, Grandma would say, "It's okay. She's learning. Remember, she's only two." This support really helped Mom through the tense moments.

If Winona went a little in her panties, but then made it to the bathroom to finish in the toilet, she'd still get a sticker. She was completely trained in five days. Nikki was so pleased.

TOILETING ACCIDENTS

It's unrealistic to think your child will never have accidents in his colorful new underpants. When children accidentally poop or pee in their underwear, it helps them to recognize the sensation of "going." When a child realizes that he is pooping or peeing at the moment, then it follows he will soon be able to read the signals from his body that tell him he is *needing* to go. Accidents are an important part of making this body-to-mind connection.

A child must feel what it's like to actually go before he can thoughtfully control the bowel and bladder muscles long enough to reach the toilet. When children finally make this connection, you will see it written all over their faces.

During the learning process, 80% of children have setbacks. Even after potty use seems well established, be prepared for accidents during the next six months. Carry a change of clothes for the unexpected times when your child is focused on a new activity or there's no bathroom nearby.

Stories from the Bathroom

Learning from Experience *(Pablo, 3 years)*

Pablo stood on a chair at the kitchen table completing a puzzle, new underpants on, but that's all—no shoes, socks, or pants. All of the sudden, he started to pee. His eyes lighted up, he gasped and looked down to see pee running down his leg. Mom calmly responded, "Pablo, you're peeing. Let's go in the bathroom, so you can sit on the toilet. I'll clean you up." After Mom cleaned him, she set him on the toilet and said, "Next time when you feel the need to pee, tell me, and I'll take you in the bathroom so you can pee in the toilet."

After this experience Pablo knew what Mom was talking about. He still had a few accidents, but each day there were fewer.

Accidents Bring Experience *(Alex, almost 3 years)*

Janet didn't want Alex to have accidents and experience any toileting failure; she only wanted him to have success. He was bowel trained completely, but continued to pee in his diapers. Janet didn't know how to avoid accidents while urine training Alex. She consulted a child development specialist who assured her it would not damage Alex's self-esteem to have a few accidents. In fact, he needed to experience the sensation of peeing without diapers to get the idea of what this urinating business was all about.

Managing Accidents

Once training begins, don't be horrified by accidents. Be prepared for them. Corn starch dries up wet urine spots on carpets, chairs, and mattresses. If your child is sitting on the couch and wets her underpants, just put lots of corn starch on the spot, let it dry overnight, and vacuum it up the next day.

Little girls sometimes pee too far forward and wet on their panties. Help your daughter place herself far enough back on the toilet seat to get the pee in the toilet. Help her slide her panties all the way down to her ankles. In time, and with practice, she will discover a comfortable and efficient position for urinating.

Bowel accidents are messier to clean up. If your child poops in her underwear, clean her in the bathtub. Remove the soiled clothing and explain calmly, "Next time you need to poop, tell me and I'll take you to sit on the toilet."

Once you've cleaned your child up after an accident, it helps if you can get her to sit on the potty chair or toilet for a minute or so. By doing this you're helping your child make the connection that poop and pee go into the toilet. While she's sitting on the toilet, read her a story[5] about going potty, make up a silly song about peeing and pooping, or tell a story you've made up about a little child who used to pee and poop in her underpants, but now goes in the toilet.

Also be prepared when your newly trained child says she needs to go—you don't have much time. You can't ask your child to wait while you finish your shopping; you must locate a restroom right then. In time, the bowel and bladder muscles strengthen to the point where the child can hold the urine and stool in for longer periods, but at first the ability to hold it is very limited.

MORE TIPS FOR TOILETING SUCCESS

Here are some ideas and tips that will help smooth the road to toilet training.

Cleanliness

Children need to learn hygienic habits when it comes to using the toilet. They need to sit or stand carefully so the urine and stool reaches the toilet bowl. Eventually they must learn to wipe themselves, but at first they need assistance from you—especially for bowel movements. Teach girls to avoid urinary tract infections by wiping from front to back. This avoids avoid introducing bacteria into the urethra (the tube that empties the bladder).

Children need to learn to flush and then wash their hands

---

[5] Refer to the list of recommended children's stories on potty training in the Resource section.

afterwards. Make it part of the routine from the beginning. It may be a hassle to enforce, but it is an important habit to instill. The most effective approach is for parent and child to wash their hands *together*.

Teach good hygiene, but don't obsess over it. Some parents are so overly worried and anxious about germs that their children begin retaining their bowels to avoid all the fuss. Germs are like people. We are surrounded by them and most are helpful—not harmful. In healthy people, the normal bacteria in the intestines are necessary for good health and are not harmful. We wash hands because we don't know ahead of time when someone might have an infection.

Wash with plain soap, not anti-bacterial soap. Like excessive use of antibiotics, excessive use of such bactericidal soaps is a set-up for developing strains of resistant bacteria that are problematic. Such anti-bacterial soaps are also harmful to the environment.

Reminders

When you first put your child in underwear, you might offer a reminder every hour or so. "Son, do you need to pee? Let's try. I'll go with you to the bathroom." There are two cautions here. First, little ones who are at the height of the "terrible two's" (commonly about two and a half years) will almost always resist reminders with a determined, "No!" Reminders usually work better before or after this phase. Second, be careful because your child may get into the habit of depending on you to tell him when it's time to go. Eventually your child must learn to read his own body signals to discover the sensation of needing to go. So at first, ask him, "Do you feel like you need to pee or poop?"

Children at age four tend to resent any familiar, direct reminders. So before leaving the house, ask, "What do we do before getting in the car?" rather than saying "Go to the bathroom before we leave the house." Later, back off and allow your child to take the responsibility himself without reminders from you.

Bathroom Talk

Don't be surprised if you hear your child use words that refer to urine and stool in inappropriate ways and in inappropriate settings. This is common practice among children up to about age five. "He's a poo-poo head." "This soup looks like pee." The variations on the use of these words are only limited by a child's imagination, which, during the pre-school years, is fertile and unbridled. If your child notices that this talk bothers you a great deal, that will make it worse. This phase will likely pass most quickly if you simply ignore it.

On the other hand, some parents find it hard to tolerate inappropriate and over-use of references to bodily functions. If bathroom talk is a problem in your household, each time your child uses it, nonchalantly escort him to the bathroom. Tell him, "If you need to use bathroom talk, the place to do it is in the bathroom." When you get there, sit down and tell your child that you will listen. Don't act shocked; just listen. When your child is finished, ask him, "Are you finished using bathroom talk now? If you need to use those words again, let me know. I'll come to the bathroom with you any time to listen." This approach defuses the negative attention such words can bring. Bathroom talk quickly drops out of sight—at least in your presence.

TRAVELING WITH NEW TRAINEES

Remember that even when you are "finished" with potty training, accidents are common within the first six months, especially when anything differs from your child's usual routine.

When you take your newly trained child out somewhere, always take an extra set of clothes with you. Many children won't pee in strange toilets at shopping malls and restaurants. They only want to pee in their very own toilet. Some parents take a portable potty seat with them during this period. Other parents remind the child, "We can go potty here, even though we aren't at home." It won't be too long, however, before your son or daughter will want to try out every toilet available, whether you're at a friend's house or a gas station.

Here are more useful tips and techniques to make toileting away from home easier.

- Always carry a change of clothes with you, just in case.
- Many families spend a lot of time in the car. Place a diaper on the car seat to protect it from accidents. Carry a tightly covered con-

tainer in the car as an emergency potty.

- When you first arrive somewhere, point out or visit the public restroom before you actually need it. This helps those kids who don't like surprises.

- When using public restrooms, you can take either gender child with you to your bathroom through age four. (Dad can quickly carry his daughter to a private stall in the men's room.) Starting at age five, wait outside the door of the opposite-gender restroom for your child.

- To avoid your child becoming frightened by the unexpected "whoosh" of an automatic flush toilet beneath him or her, hold your hand, or drape a paper towel over the "electric eye" until you are ready to leave.

- If you'll be at an event with an adult-sized, portable restroom, and your child would be distressed by that big open hole, take along a portable potty seat to put on top.

- If your child is unable to poop in a public restroom, be sure to allow some extra time to relax and use the potty once you get home.

GETTING STARTED CHECKLIST

If your child is ready physically, emotionally, socially, and intellectually, *do these four steps simultaneously:*

- ☐ Set aside a block of time in your busy life to begin training.
- ☐ Buy a potty chair or an insert to fit on the big toilet, if you haven't already done so.
- ☐ Take your child to buy underwear.
- ☐ Establish two potty-sitting practice sessions a day. Leave diapers on. (This step is necessary only if your child isn't naturally interested in toileting.)

If your child is cooperative:

- ☐ Take diapers off for practice sessions, but don't expect performance.

If your child continues to cooperate and her interest is piqued, proceed by choosing one of the three approaches—Part-Time, Child's Choice, or Full-Time Potty Training.

The time frame for achieving training success is difficult to predict. Some children experience immediate success—after a week they are confident toilet users. Other children make slower, but definite progress. If, after a month, your child still has lots of accidents, it's time to reevaluate his readiness, possibly return to diapers, and allow him a little more time to mature.

4

To Reward or Not to Reward: That's the Question

Ethan sits on the potty holding his bear. Dad smiles with approval and calls to Mom, "Look at Ethan. He's sitting on the potty." Tameeka pees in the toilet and Mom gives her a sticker; when she poops, she gets an M&M®. Alma announces to Juliana's older brother and sister that she just pooped for the first time in the little potty chair they once used. They run to the bathroom to see. These situations are all examples of rewards that encourage children to learn to use the toilet.

Smiles, hugs, applause, and positive statements, such as, "Good for you, you're sitting on your little toilet while Mom sits on the big toilet!" are social rewards. These kinds of social rewards are necessary for training all children. Candy, trinkets, or stickers for toileting efforts or results are tangible rewards. Such tangible rewards can be used effectively to accomplish toileting tasks, but they are not essential for every child.

SOCIAL REWARDS

Think about the positive attention you focus on your child as he learns to walk. It is so exciting to watch a child take those first brave steps and eventually toddle across the room. You automatically pay positive attention to your child as he makes any minor advancement toward confident walking. When he falls, you don't scold. You just wait and watch until he's ready to try again. When he does try again, you naturally turn, watch, smile, clap, and focus on him as he works on this skill.

When you watch your child walk for the first time at thirteen months, you don't think about little Sara down the street who walked at nine months. When a child walks, it's the time that's right for him and that's what is important.

As your toddler shows off this new skill, you're proud of him, but you know the accomplishment is his alone. You provided an environment that supports walking: a sturdy floor and a safe place to practice. You also provided emotional and social support, that is, positive attention and encouragement. As he becomes an accomplished walker, you no longer need to cheer every step he takes around the house. The same forms of social rewards used for walking can be adapted when guiding your child to use the toilet.

Children need positive attention focused on each baby step they make toward success. Educating your child to use the toilet is a bit more complicated than attending to him as he learns to walk. With walking, you know to just wait and watch and it will happen. In toilet instruction, your role is to prompt and encourage your child as she makes the transition from diapers to underpants. You need to watch and show interest with no expectation for immediate success. Your child also needs you to suggest—and sometimes sensitively impose—the next step to toileting independence. Your role is trickier, but the positive reinforcement you provide is the same.

Positive Responses that Encourage Toileting Success

- **Notice.** "I saw your teddy bear on the toilet. He likes to sit there."
- **Show love.** Get down on the child's level. Establish eye contact and give your child happy, approving looks as he sits on the toilet.
- **Talk or read together.** Make sitting on the potty or the big toilet a relaxed and enjoyable time.
- **Describe what she's doing.** "You're grunting. You're trying to push a poop into the toilet. Way to go."
- **Give praise.** Clap briefly, or say, "You peed in your potty chair! Good for you. You look proud and happy. Mom and Dad are proud and happy too."

- **Tell others.** Call Dad or Grandma on the phone and share any toileting success. Encourage your child to make the call or let your child overhear your conversation.

CONTINUE POSITIVE PATTERNS

Diaper changing is usually a positive time for a parent and child. You make eye contact, talk, and laugh. One-on-one positive attention is focused totally on the child. Parents need to continue this same level of focus and positive attention as the child gives up diapers and works toward toileting independence.

Stories from the Bathroom

Attention Counts *(Braden, 2 years, 9 months)*

Diaper changing had always been a fun time for Kate and her son Braden. Mom would tell silly stories as she changed Braden's diapers. Then, with toilet instruction, this special time dropped out of sight. Braden seemed ready intellectually and physically, but he wasn't making much progress.

Suddenly a light went on for Kate. She enticed Braden to use the toilet with the promise of hearing one of the silly stories she told him when she changed his diapers. This was the key. She stopped the stories for diaper changes, but told them when he practiced or performed on the toilet.

Braden had missed the stories and the attention they brought from Mom. When the stories and attention resumed while Braden sat on the toilet, he made progress quickly.

The point is obvious. Give your child the same amount of attention for potty training as you did for diaper changing, and success will occur in a more timely fashion.

REINFORCE THE POSITIVE, NOT THE NEGATIVE

If you give children attention for their positive actions, they continue to behave positively. If you pay too much attention to misbehavior, you'll see children continuing to misbehave. Negative attention includes trying to talk children out of their inappropriate behavior.

If your child refuses to sit on the toilet, don't ask, "Why won't you sit on the potty?" and don't go on and on about the importance of learning the task. Parents often over-explain toileting procedures, as if thinking the child will eventually say, "I get it. No problem. I'll poop in the toilet since you explained it so well." These attempts to convince your child draw too much negative attention to the topic and seldom influence behavior positively.

Instead, just say, "I know you don't want to practice, but you need to sit on the toilet for thirty seconds." Proceed, being firm and kind, but clear about what you expect. Then praise any effort made. "You tried— good for you."

Coercive tactics—"What will Grandma think when she comes to visit next week and you're not peeing in the toilet?"—are confusing to a child and will hinder toileting success. Negative comments and rhetorical questions—"You peed your pants again? When are you going to grow up?"—serve no purpose either.

If children get positive attention for toileting attempts and successes, they usually progress in a timely way, correct for their developing bodies. If they get negative reinforcement for toileting accidents or for not progressing on your preferred schedule, it will most likely hinder their progress.

There's no need for negative comments or body language that communicates unhappiness or disgust. If you have a very sensitive nose and find messy diapers hard to tolerate, breathe through your mouth so the odors are less intense.

Negative Responses that Hinder Toileting Success

- **Labeling**. "Big girls don't wear diapers. Are you going to be a baby your whole life?"
- **Comparing**. "Your friend Carter wears underpants and he's younger than you." "All your friends are trained—don't you want to be trained too?"
- **Reinforcing the negative.** "Another accident? Why do you keep doing this?"
- **Negative body language.** Scowling, glaring, shaking your head,

looking very disappointed, disgusted, or disapproving when your child isn't progressing as you expect.
- **Scolding or yelling**. "You're too old and too big to be wearing diapers," or "You make me so angry! I don't like it when you poop in your underpants!"

Parenting would be easy if such negative comments actually changed children's behavior for the better. Unfortunately, this is rarely the case. Disapproving statements typically leave children paralyzed and not knowing how to change their behavior. Since they don't know *what* to do, or how to do it, they simply keep on behaving in the same old negative fashion.

COMMUNICATE CLEARLY

There will be times during toilet training when it is appropriate for you to let your child know how you feel and what you expect. Try using an I-Statement: 1) Use the pronoun "I", 2) explain how you feel, 3) precisely describe the behavior you approve of or disapprove of, and 4) then tell your child what you expect.

Examples:
- "I'm so happy you're wearing your pretty new underwear. Remember, you're not supposed to pee or poop in them."
- "I'm tired of changing dirty diapers. I hope you learn to poop in the toilet soon."
- "I'm disappointed you wet your underwear at preschool today. Please try to remember to use the toilet."
- "I'm angry. I don't want you to pee in your brother's baseball cap. You need to pee in the toilet."
- "I'm so proud of you! You pooped in the toilet. I'll bet you'll do it again tomorrow."

Positive comments are most effective at helping your child succeed. Negative responses usually work against improving toileting behavior and can harm your child's emotional well-being. When your child does have an accident or setback, it's usually best to clean your child up in a matter-of-fact fashion. There is no need to establish eye contact or talk.

Just clean the child and then evaluate his readiness for training. Do you continue with your plan? Do you change the plan? Do you put your child back in diapers?

Always remember, ultimate control lies with the child. It's her body and she's in control. You have lots of influence, but it only goes so far. Your best tools are positive social rewards for each baby step your child makes toward learning to use the toilet.

IMAGINATIVE REWARDS

Children have wonderful imaginations. You can use this fact to make toileting more fun for kids, even if the ideas sound silly to adults.

Examples:
- Vincent's mother encouraged him this way, "The toilet *loves* poops. Do you have any poops to make the toilet happy today?"
- Grandma excitedly said, "LeShawn, there's a fire in the toilet—you better run and put it out." LeShawn's face lit up and his imagination took over. At that moment, he was a fire fighter. He ran into the bathroom and peed, pretending to be at the scene of a big fire.
- Juliana named her poops. The big ones were daddy poops, the middle-sized ones were mommy poops, and the tiny ones were baby poops. She'd wave "Bye-bye" to her family of poops as she flushed them down the toilet.
- Emily loved her princess panties. Her mom made this remark, "Emily, now remember, you don't want to get any pee or poop on the princess." When Emily had an accident, Mom said calmly, "Oh, no, you pooped on the princess. She doesn't like poop on her and hopes you'll poop in the toilet next time." Mom was careful not to shame Emily, but the comment helped motivate her to toileting success.

TANGIBLE REWARDS

Tangible rewards don't have to be expensive to be effective. There are many ways to use trinkets and other items to motivate children.

Examples:

- Drop a piece of toilet paper in the potty and ask, "Can you make it wet?"
- If you put blue food coloring in the toilet, it will turn green as your child pees. Some children think this is magical.
- With boys, drop a square of toilet paper in the toilet for target practice. Targets make it fun and improve the boy's aim.
- It's common practice for parents to reward children with a small snack, such as a goldfish cracker or a fruit snack, when they urinate in the toilet. Parents can also reward with a small toy when they have a bowel movement in the toilet.
- Consider using a star chart (described on page 121).

> *Warning:*
> If a child is not physically developed enough, to the point where he can hold in his urine or stool and then release it into the toilet, a tangible reward system will not work and it is not fair to use this tactic. You would be expecting a child to do something for which he lacks the physical maturity. So be certain if you try rewarding a child with trinkets that he's developed enough physically to accomplish the task.

Some children may go too far to get a reward. One mom found her daughter grunting and straining, trying to force out a poop just to get an M&M®. Mom told her, "I don't want you to push; wait until it's ready." This little bit of coaching took care of the problem.

Some children respond positively to such tangible rewards. A trinket for success helps get them over the hump of transitioning from diapers to underwear. It depersonalizes the process and offers the child a choice. The child is not using the toilet to please her mom or dad; she's using it to get the reward. Whenever children have a choice in a situation, it gives them power and control. Here's an example of how a reward system provided just that feeling of control.

Stories from the Bathroom

Reward Succeeds *(Joshua, 3 years)*

Joshua loved the colorful little plastic cars that were displayed in large jars at the drug store. He always begged for one. Joshua was also having a little trouble with training. A power struggle was starting to build between him and his mother. Mom would ask him to sit on the toilet. Typically, he'd stomp his foot and yell, "No, no!"

Then Mom told him he couldn't watch TV until he tried to pee or poop on the toilet. Joshua didn't care. He just sat on the floor and played with his cars and usually wet or pooped his pants.

Mom knew her son was socially, intellectually, and physically ready, but for some reason she couldn't get him to go in the toilet. There was a push–pull going on between the two that both could feel. So Mom tried a reward system.

She said, "Joshua, I bought a jar of these plastic cars at the drug store today. You have a choice: You can go potty in the toilet and get one of these plastic cars, or you can choose to pee in your underwear. It's fine with me if you go in your underwear, but when you do, you won't get one of these cars."

Joshua was dry for up to two hours, so Mom knew he had control. When he had an accident in his underwear, all Mom said was, "You peed in your underwear. Remember, when you go in the toilet, you'll get one of these." She pointed to the jar full of plastic cars displayed in the bathroom. When Joshua did go in the toilet, he picked a car from the jar.

After two or three days, he was doing great. He was dry most of the day and had collected several cars. He became so skilled that he could stop and start peeing with amazing control. So he tried this: He peed a little into the toilet and chose a car from the jar. Fifteen minutes later, he was back in the bathroom going a little more for another car. Mom caught on quickly to his scheme. She said, "You must empty your bladder to get a car.

—continued on next page

—continued from previous page

I'll watch you pee to see if you've completely emptied your bladder."

Once the colorful plastic cars in the jar were gone, the reward system was over. Did Joshua start peeing his pants again? Not at all. He was accustomed to having dry pants. The reward system helped him make the transition from peeing and pooping in his underwear to doing so in the toilet. There was no need to buy more cars, or to up the ante with more enticing rewards.

A reward must be immediate. The child must get the trinket as soon as she performs. A plan that requires a child to stay dry and clean for a week before getting the reward won't work. A week is too long in the life of a child. It's best to give a little reward each time the child pees or poops into the toilet.

If you want to give a more substantial reward than a trinket, then you can use a chart and sticker system. The child earns a star or sticker every time she performs in the toilet. Once she earns ten stickers, she gets the reward (toy). Do not remove stickers for accidents; that's far too discouraging and will sabotage the whole process.

There is another factor important for the successful use of rewards. It must be something the child *really* wants. If you try to motivate a child with stickers when what she really loves are marshmallows, you're wasting your time. She has to sincerely want the reward you're offering.

Stories from the Bathroom

Pennies for Pee *(Shameeka, 2 years 9 months)*

Shameeka was negative about everything—which is common for a child her age. She steered clear of the potty chair in the bathroom, avoid-

—continued on next page

—continued from previous page

ing it at all costs. Her mom, Rhonda, knew Shameeka had bladder control because she woke up dry every morning. Once, Rhonda gently placed Shameeka on her potty chair. The result was a 30-minute temper tantrum. Afterwards Shameeka wouldn't even enter the bathroom; her mom had to carry her in there for a bath.

Rhonda noticed that Shameeka loved pennies. She had five and played with them every day. She would put them in a purse, carry them around for a while, then transfer the coins to another purse.

One day Shameeka asked her mother for another penny. Opportunity knocked. Rhonda said, "You can have a penny, but you must sit on your little potty chair first." It worked. Shameeka ran to the bathroom and sat for a few seconds on her potty chair with her purse and pennies in hand. She was not required to perform; she did not even have to take off her diaper. Rhonda awarded Shameeka her penny, which she promptly added to her collection.

Rhonda and Shameeka continued this routine all day. Shameeka collected about ten more pennies. The next day Rhonda told her she could get a penny only if she sat on the potty while Mom read her a short story. Shameeka collected five more pennies that day.

The following day, Rhonda told Shameeka she could have ten pennies if she'd wear panties. Shameeka agreed. That morning she sat on the potty and peed as Rhonda read her a story. Shameeka was on her way to being trained.

The next day Rhonda went to the bank to obtain a roll of brand new pennies. She showed the pennies to her daughter, who was dazzled by their newness and sparkle. Rhonda simply explained, "Today, and from now on, you will receive a penny when you pee or poop in your potty chair." Shameeka did have a few accidents, but the penny plan was tremendously effective. Soon, she was completely trained. Rhonda continued to offer the pennies with each success in the toilet until the pennies ran out.

Two year olds, with their negative attitudes, are often resistant to using the toilet at first, because it means compliance. At two, children are pushing for independence and exercising their own control; compliance symbolizes dependency. Shameeka, in the example above, worked for pennies, which put *her* in control of the process.

Stories from the Bathroom

Play with the Big Kids *(Chaske, 3 years)*

Chaske could use the potty, but didn't pay attention to his "need to go" sensations when he was involved in play. So his mom made some new rules. If she found him outside with wet pants, he had to come in and play in the house by himself for fifteen minutes. If he wet three pairs of pants in one day, she told him he'd used up all the clean ones so he'd have to stay inside for the rest of the day. Chaske loved playing outside with his brother and the other big kids, so that gave him lots of incentive. Within a couple of weeks, he was routinely dry all day.

Social rewards are essential to toilet training children. Tangible rewards can be very useful, but are not always necessary. Use your knowledge of your child to decide whether to use tangible rewards to motivate training.

WHEN REWARDS DON'T WORK

Sometimes a reward system helps, as in the stories above, and sometimes it backfires, complicating the toileting process. For example, Anthony, in the next story, was not interested in any reward offered by Mom or Dad.

Stories from the Bathroom

Reward Fails *(Anthony, 3 years)*

Anthony was a child determined to train himself in his very own way and time. Mom secretly thought that if he tried wearing underwear just once, he'd realize they weren't so bad after all and he might start wearing them full-time. One day she suggested to Anthony that she'd buy him the Lego® set he really wanted if he'd wear underwear for just one hour of one day. No way. Anthony refused the offer. This surprised Mom, who knew that Anthony would really love the Lego® set she offered.

Rewards don't work for every child. If a power struggle is brewing, as might be the case for Anthony and his mom, then rewards are unlikely to help. Chapter 6 offers more help with this potty training problem.

5

When Your Plan Doesn't Succeed

What if, for whatever reason, your attempts to toilet train your child are not successful? Even though you have read, planned, placed a potty chair in your bathroom, and purchased cute underwear for her, she still has accident after accident. Days go by and there's no toileting success. You try rewarding her with candy, but she's not interested. You try sitting her on the toilet every hour and she's willing to try, but ends up tense, in tears, and never manages to get one drop in the toilet. Then, minutes later, her underpants are wet again.

Despite the fact you thought she was ready physically, emotionally, intellectually, and socially—after all she is two and a half—it's clear she just isn't ready. If, after four to six days of struggles and accidents, you don't observe *any* progress or interest from your child, back off, put diapers back on, and try again in a couple of months.

On the other hand, if your child is slow to catch on, but you sense she is making baby steps toward training, keep at it. Consistent control just takes longer for some children than others. Your child may require more time to perceive the sensation of needing to go and may need a longer time to gain conscious control of the bowel and bladder muscles. Putting the child who is making gradual progress back in diapers would spell defeat and negate any minor success she'd already had.

PHYSICAL REASONS FOR LONGER—OR LATER—TRAINING

Before returning your child to diapers, observe your child's general muscle tone. Are your child's muscles generally relaxed? Or does he have muscles that are usually tight and quick to respond? Children with loose, relaxed muscles may have trouble holding tight while getting to the bathroom. Children with very tight muscles may have trouble relaxing and letting go once they get there. Toileting is easiest for children in the middle of the muscle spectrum. With either extreme, toilet learning may take a little longer. This is one reason why some children need only a week to catch on and others take a month or more. Your child may just need more time to practice and learn, rather than a return to diapers.

Some children are less aware of body sensations. Invite them to place their hands on their lower belly. Say, "That is where you'll feel it when you need to pee or poop. What do you feel inside there now?"

When your child is in diapers, she may squat to urinate or have a bowel movement. Other children may sit in a chair or stand. Another child may have a bowel movement only when relaxed after a nap or right after a bath. When you start educating your child to use the toilet, you are introducing a new environment. Suddenly, she is required to sit on the toilet, without diapers, to poop or pee. The difference in surroundings and positions takes some adjustment on your child's part. So be patient as your child learns to use his or her muscles in a new way and in a new place. Both boys and girls must figure out how to hold muscles tight while getting to the toilet, then how to relax those muscles to pee. When they get to the toilet to poop, they have to tighten their abdominal muscles for pushing and, at the same time, relax the muscles around the anus. Using the toilet can feel quite different from their old diaper-protected positions.

Some children have a difficult time relaxing. This was the case in the following story.

Stories from the Bathroom

Help to Relax *(Jamie, 2 years, 10 months)*

Jamie insisted on standing to pee, but he'd just stand there and stand there; he could never relax enough to pee in the toilet. Mom and Dad knew Jamie had physical control because he'd wake up dry each morning.

Jamie's morning routine was to wake up and sit on his mom's lap for a story. One morning his mom said, "I'll read you your story while you stand at the toilet and try to pee." That's all it took. As she read Jamie the story, he finally relaxed and peed into the toilet.

MISSING BODY MESSAGES

Once schooling a child to use the toilet is officially underway, it usually takes only three or four days to sense if your child is catching on to the training regime. After a month, the process should be fairly well established.

It's difficult for many children to focus on play activity *and* listen to the body's messages about the need to go. Some children playing outside don't want to miss out on any fun, so they put off trips to the bathroom for too long. They don't give themselves enough time to run inside and end up wetting their pants. Some boys remedy this easily by sneaking off to pee behind a tree; for girls, this approach is less convenient, so they usually learn to run into the house for quick trips to the bathroom.

Most children do need reminders. Occasionally parents get in the habit of too frequently reminding their child about visiting the bathroom and then escorting their child there. This is okay to begin with, but if you continue to make frequent reminders and take your child to the toilet, at some point you need to back off and let him assume this responsibility himself. He needs to listen to the signals from his body that tell him it's time to go. Yes, he might have an accident or two, but that's typically all it takes to master the process.

DANGEROUS SHORTCUTS

You will sometimes hear about "shortcuts" to manage toileting. There can be serious health risks involved. For example, some parents inappropriately rely on laxatives to get their child on a predictable elimination schedule. Using laxatives unnecessarily, or for too long, can diminish the body's natural ability to pass stool. Always consult with your child's doctor before using laxatives.

Other parents, unwilling to be inconvenienced by lots of potty stops, tell a child to "hold it" for long periods of time. Holding excess urine in the bladder is painful and may cause harmful back-flow into the kidneys. Practical solutions are better for your child's health, such as: routinely using the bathroom before a car ride, carrying a covered container for use in the car, and making any necessary potty stops.

Some parents tell stories of dramatically reducing the fluids a child drinks in order to decrease visits to the bathroom. Although it is reasonable to limit the amount of water a child drinks before bedtime, be sure your child gets enough liquid during the day. For more information on liquid needs, see Chapter 3, page 45.

A TEMPORARY RETURN TO DIAPERS

If you ease off and your child doesn't take over the responsibility of toileting, consider putting diapers back on. You can make another attempt in a couple of months. It's easier to return to diapers and wait until the child is ready than it is to struggle with accidents month after month. Your child won't be devastated; in fact, most children who have lots of accidents feel relief returning to diapers because the pressure is off. The child can relax, have more time to grow in the four important areas of developmental readiness, and then try again later.

Here's all you need to say, "You know, we've tried teaching you to use the toilet and you keep wetting and pooping in your underpants. I think we'll put your diapers back on and try again in a couple of months. Someday you'll go in the toilet, but for now, I think it's time to go back to diapers."

If you do this, don't stop all the pre-toilet training activities you were doing before you introduced wearing underpants. Keep the potty chair in the bathroom. Unless your child protests or struggles repeatedly, put her on the toilet twice a day. This is just to practice sitting without any expectation of results. You can also set your child on the potty or toilet for a moment after you remove each wet or poopy diaper. Encourage your child to take stuffed animals and dolls to sit on the potty. You're not forgetting about educating your child to use the toilet just because you've returned to diapers. Your child isn't ready for underpants, but the toileting orientation process continues.

Stories from the Bathroom

Back to Diapers *(Tyler, 2 years)*

Nichole decided to start steering Tyler to use the toilet right after he turned two. When she noticed Tyler start to strain and grunt, she'd scoop him up, set him on the toilet, and he'd go without any problem. Soon Tyler was telling his mom when he needed to poop and off they'd go to the bathroom. He'd poop in his little potty chair and then empty the poop into the big toilet and flush. He really enjoyed this whole process.

Urinating was different; here, they had no luck. Tyler simply was not interested. They had potty chairs in every room. Tyler put his Buddy doll on the potty chairs but he never tried to pee there. Nichole tried everything. She threatened, "If you don't use the toilet, no TV." She tried rewards, "When you pee in the toilet, you'll get a candy."

Finally, Nichole consulted with Tyler's pediatrician. He said to return Tyler to diapers and wait. Tyler walked late, at about 18 months. Because of the delay with walking, the doctor pointed out that this slow-down might affect Tyler's ability to learn to use the toilet too. So Nichole took the doctor's advice and put Tyler in disposable training pants so he could get them up and down easily for bowel movements, yet have protection for peeing.

—continued on next page

—continued from previous page

The summer Tyler turned three, Nichole set out to train him again. She was a college student and had the summer off, so it was the ideal time to train. This time it all seemed to come together for Tyler. His mom dressed him in easy-to-remove clothes and underpants. She asked him frequently, "Do you need to pee?" Every time she used the toilet herself, she took Tyler with her.

Nichole was a single parent with one older daughter, so Tyler had no male role model around the house on a daily basis. But when Dad or Grandpa did come for a visit, she asked them to take Tyler with them to the bathroom so he could watch and try for himself.

At first Tyler had up to seven accidents a day, but he made gradual progress. At the beginning of August, he started to tell his mom, "I need to pee."

When Nichole returned to college at the end of September, Tyler was doing fairly well, but still needed reminders, and was having occasional accidents. Nichole would run to the child care center between classes to take Tyler to the toilet. She worried that in this busy and stimulating center, Tyler would forget about urinating in the toilet. After a month, she no longer needed to stop at the center between classes; Tyler was noticing when he needed to go and telling the child care providers.

At five and a half, Tyler continued to need diapers at night. The doctor reassured Nichole that for Tyler, this wasn't surprising; as in the other areas of development, this also would take a little longer. In time, he would train through the night and there was little she could do to speed the process.

Nichole's approach in the above story was admirable. She combined patience, determination, and sensitivity to reach the desired goal. Nichole and Tyler had a tougher and longer training period than most do, but more importantly, Tyler learned to use the toilet in the way that was right for him.

REGRESSION AND FAMILY STRESS

Regression occurs when a child appears trained for two weeks or more and then reverts to having repeated accidents. It can happen when the child wasn't truly all-the-way ready in the first place or as a result of stress.

It is commonplace for children under two years old (or those who are slightly over two), to appear trained, when, in actuality, they were not fully ready in the beginning. They want to please their parents, so they work hard and really concentrate on not having accidents. Soon they discover that toileting feels like a lot of work; it requires too much time and concentration. Then they start having accidents.

If this is the case with your child, don't panic. Get out those diapers again and realize it's temporary. Your child just needs a little more time to mature.

Stories from the Bathroom

Waiting for Readiness *(Emma, 2½ years)*

Emma appeared trained; for two weeks she had no accidents. Then she had a few wetting incidents. Mom didn't scold her, but was very disappointed when Emma wet her underpants. Then Mom noticed some changes in Emma's behavior. She stopped playing spontaneously; she just sat quietly on the floor looking worried and occupied about when it might be time to pee in the toilet. Mom sensed the stress Emma was experiencing from trying to stay dry and put her back in diapers.

Emma continued to poop in the toilet, but it wasn't until her third birthday that Mom put her back in panties. She trained very quickly on this second try.

Another factor to consider before introducing toilet training, or when the process stalls, is your family's stress level. Any stress can cause regression. If your child is trained and then begins having accidents, look at what stress might exist in her immediate environment. Is there a new baby in the house—or one imminent? Has Grandpa just moved in for three months? Are you getting ready to move across the street or across the country? Has your older child just started school and suddenly disappeared from your preschooler's day? Are you in the process of getting a divorce? Is your child starting or changing child care situations? Are you starting a new job that will change your child's schedule?

Any of these factors, or more, adds stress to your child's life and can hinder his ability to learn to use the toilet. Most families live with some stress daily, but if there's any new glaring change that is going to take time and adjustment on your child's part (or yours), wait until life calms down before jumping into toileting education.

Guiding your child takes concentration, persistence, and patience on your part. If you're adjusting to a new job, or your spouse has just been laid off, wait for a little bit. Starting the toileting process now might set your child up for failure and you may be simply setting yourself up for frustration.

Too many changes imposed on children at once usually hinder their success. Learning to control the bowel and bladder muscles is a necessary frustration children endure. But if this learning process is forced on top of other stresses, children may become too anxious to succeed.

On the other hand, if your *child* is eager to train, even if a big change like a new sibling is going to happen soon, go ahead and train. The child can learn to use the toilet, but expect some regression when the baby actually arrives. The re-learning process goes quickly and the window of opportunity for learning hasn't slipped by.

Stories from the Bathroom

Return to Diapers like Baby Sister (Diego, almost 3 years)

Diego was completely trained one month before his new baby sister arrived. Maritza was reluctant to train him, but Diego was interested, willing, and completely ready. It was a snap. When the new baby arrived on the scene, Diego accepted this intrusion willingly at first. Then, after a few days, he asked, "When is that baby going back to the hospital?" Mom

—continued on next page

—continued from previous page

explained that baby Elvita would not be going back to the hospital. She was a member of the family now and would be living with them forever. Once this realization sunk in, Diego started wetting his underpants two or three times a day.

This was not what Mom needed—a new baby and a toddler who wet the carpet, couch, or floor twice a day. Maritza was horrified. She pleaded with Diego to use the toilet, asked him why he was doing it, and told him only babies wet their pants, not big boys like Diego. With each accident, Mom scolded Diego and sent him to his bedroom. The accidents started to escalate.

Finally, Maritza consulted a child development specialist. Her advice was to put Diego back in diapers. This new baby in the family added stress to Diego's life and he responded by wetting his pants. She encouraged Maritza to look at the situation from Diego's perspective. When his baby sister was born, Diego lost some of the positive attention he was accustomed to getting from Maritza. Diego discovered that wetting his pants got him the quick attention—even though negative—he was craving from his mom. Maritza's emotional response contributed to the more persistent wetting.

It took about a month of being back in diapers before Diego decided, on his own, to return to underpants. During this time Diego had adjusted somewhat to life with his new baby sister.

The stress factor contributes to toileting regression. If your child regresses due to a new change in the family, simply clean up the accidents (encouraging your child to help as much as she is able) without scolding or shaming her. Don't call too much negative attention to the problem or get hysterical or disgusted. If your child's regression causes you to become emotional and out-of-control, this only compounds the problem. It can be downright interesting—even exciting—for children to see parents hysterical; few can resist provoking you by peeing on the floor to get that emotional response.

For this reason, if your child starts having accidents, it's important that your response be low key. You need to spend your energy on pinpointing the source of the problem. Decide what you can or can't do to relieve the stress. Time is often the best remedy; consider putting her in diapers or disposable training pants until the stress is over and then go through the teaching process again. Don't panic; most likely the second try will be almost effortless.

Regression may also be the result of a medical problem. If your child has persistent setbacks, it's always a good idea to consult with your physician.

CAN I HAVE A DIAPER, PLEASE?

Another common occurrence is for a child to be completely urine trained, but to ask for a diaper when it's time to poop. This is what happened with Elizabeth in the story below.

Stories from the Bathroom

Have Diaper, Will Poop *(Elizabeth, 2 ½ years)*

Mom couldn't believe it. Elizabeth was wearing pretty new panties and going into the bathroom on her own to urinate, but insisting on a diaper when it was time to poop. How could this be? And why?

Mom complied with her child's request for a diaper. Elizabeth had managed urine training almost totally on her own, so Mom decided to trust her need for a diaper for bowel movements. Two weeks passed before, all on her own, Elizabeth started pooping in the toilet.

Remember, urine training and bowel training are two separate processes. Often children learn one skill before the other. Occasionally, training occurs concurrently, but many children respond as Elizabeth did, insisting on a diaper when it's time to poop. If your child is asking for a diaper for bowel movements, go ahead and provide the diaper; refusing it may lead to bowel retention or a power struggle. Very few children request diapers indefinitely—most naturally move toward the bathroom.

If, after several months, your child hasn't made any progress, start gently imposing two potty-sitting practice times a day (as described in Chapter 3). See also the anecdote about Jamahl in Chapter 6 (p.91).

FEARS

Some children fear that if their stool falls into the toilet, everything else inside them will drop out as well. Others imagine they have a baby inside their tummy that will fall into the toilet. Remember, children's thinking is limited by their development; they can't yet reason the way adults do. When a child gets such a frightening notion in her head, it's difficult to talk her out of it. Use empathy first, "I know you're scared to use the toilet. Pooping seems scary to you." Now explain, "When you use the toilet, only poop and pee fall out of your body." If your child is afraid she'll be flushed away, validate the fear, but reassure your child, "Only pee, poop, and toilet paper flush down the toilet—not people." One Mom finally reassured her frightened two year old by putting a basket ball in the toilet, then flushing; he could see the ball would not go down the drain.

Stories from the Bathroom

Strong Will, Strong Fear *(Willie, 16 months to 4 years)*

Alicia placed a potty chair in the bathroom for Willie. He would sit on it when his older sister used the large toilet. Then, for no apparent reason, he started to avoid the potty chair altogether. Mom thought he was afraid of his poop dropping out of him and into the toilet. Willie coped with his fears by avoiding the toilet altogether.

According to Alicia, Willie had always been a difficult child to manage; she described him as strong-willed. He couldn't be pushed or even nudged when it came to dressing himself or cleaning up toys. Toileting instruction was no different; she met with lots of resistance from Willie.

Willie was also fastidious about cleanliness. He

—continued on next page

—continued from previous page

never used paint, hardly touched play dough, and didn't like to touch gooey foods. He disliked poop and pee equally. He was an orderly child, lining up cars and toys neatly in rows, and organizing his bedroom beyond what seemed typical for a young child.

Willie protested each of Alicia's attempts to train him. It was clear he had absolutely no interest in using the toilet. So when his third birthday approached, Mom enrolled him in a preschool that didn't require children be toilet trained.

At preschool, Willie was impressed by a friend's underpants. Although he couldn't quite bring himself to wear underwear, he consented to wear disposable training pants. After one bowel accident, Willie started pooping in the toilet. At three and a half, he still wore the training diapers because he refused to pee in the toilet.

Alicia knew from Willie's temperament that if she made even a slight hint about using the toilet, it would cause an obstinate setback in his progress. She realized that he was proceeding in small steps and was prompted only by his own interest and desire.

Even though Willie was bowel trained, he wouldn't use strange toilets. He was also soaked each morning, but Alicia didn't push nighttime dryness at all. Willie wouldn't wear underpants and couldn't even tolerate them in his dresser drawer. She knew that someday he would wear underpants, but when this happened, it would be his decision and no one else's.

Alicia had no trouble teaching her older daughter to use the toilet. So Willie's reluctance surprised her at first. She soon discovered success occurred only when she completely dropped out of the picture. Her role became that of an interested, supportive observer. Willie continued to observe his Dad and friends in preschool.

One evening when he was four and a half, Willie stepped up to the toilet and peed before getting in the bathtub. The next morning, he peed when he got up. He then marched to his bedroom, pointed to the training pants and complained, "Why are those in my room? I need real underpants!" Mom pulled his underpants out of the hall closet. Willie put on a pair for school that day and every day after that. He never had an accident.

Toilet training troubles and fears are varied and complex. The solution to many of these problems is a temporary return to diapers and a one-to-three month wait before resuming training. If you feel your frustration level rising and you're unable to discover a solution on your own, consult your pediatrician, a child development specialist, or a parent educator for ideas and help.

6

Unplugging Power Struggles

A **power struggle is an** emotional battle between parent and child over who is in control. Power struggles can happen over a wide variety of issues. Just to name a few, there's the getting dressed power struggle, the car seat power struggle, and the daily struggle to get out the door on time. When such a power play ends, usually nothing is resolved, and the same battle occurs again and again.

Potty training power struggles occur when parents invest too much of their own emotions in educating their child to use the toilet. For successful guidance, parents need a clear idea of where their influence begins and ends. Keep in mind that your child is a separate individual and ultimate control lies with her. You can put your children in bed, but you can't control when they actually fall asleep. You can provide nutritious and tasty food, but you can't make them swallow it. Likewise, you can entice and encourage children to use the toilet, but you can't make them go. Your influence is limited. Parents who cross the line to forceful and emotional tactics often end up in power struggles—emotional tug-of-wars over control.

INAPPROPRIATE PRESSURE FROM PARENTS

Parents may apply inappropriate pressure emotionally or physically. Some parents try manipulation, "Big boys go in the toilet. Only babies pee and poop in diapers. Are you going to be a baby your whole life?" Parents use this line to encourage their child to mature and use the toilet, but it usually backfires. Children already feel torn between growing up and staying little; this statement only reinforces their dilemma.

Stories from the Bathroom

Parent Tries to Force Child (Zach, 2 years)

Zach refused to poop in the toilet. Dad actually tied him to the toilet and told him to sit there until he pooped. Zach sat an hour, crying and screaming, but didn't have a bowel movement. Finally, Dad untied Zach. Fortunately, he realized this was abusive and unproductive to toilet training.

In the past, some parents would spank and scream at their children to bring results on the toilet. According to Alison Mack's book *Toilet Learning*[6], many incidents of child abuse center around toilet training. Toileting instruction sometimes becomes a battle of wills between parent and child. The parent is certain the child can poop in the toilet, but for some unknown reason, won't. The perceived willfulness triggers the parent's anger and the parent threatens the child, "If you don't poop in that toilet, I'll spank you." The child refuses, and the parent carries out the threat. This same scenario played out several times a day with escalating anger and more severe spankings amounts to child abuse.

The fact is, force, pressure, threats, and verbal or physical abuse only hurt a child's emotional well-being and delay the toilet training process. The child knows that he alone controls this process, so he digs in his heels and refuses to comply with his parents' demands. Therefore, steer away from emotional friction and tension when it comes to guiding your child to use the toilet.

---

[6] Mack, Alison. Toilet Learning. Little, Brown & Co. 1978.

Stories from the Bathroom

Power Struggle in Process *(James 2 years, 9 months)*

When Josh and Allyson started training James, he learned to urinate in the toilet quickly and easily. Bowel movements were a different story. He had a tendency toward constipation, so his bowel movements occasionally caused some pain. He didn't want to sit on the toilet for pooping.

Josh and Allyson tried every technique possible to entice James to use the toilet. First, they tried rewards: a new toy car if he pooped in the toilet. Then, punishments: a ten-minute time-out in his bedroom every time he pooped his pants. No matter what, he continued to poop in his underwear. Every week, for nine months, Josh and Allyson introduced different methods. They would start each technique with a calm demeanor, but they soon abandoned it for strong expressions of anger and exasperation. James always ended up in tears.

Their last approach was to watch James intently all day long, watching for the first strain or grunt that indicated the start of a bowel movement. When they sensed he was on the verge of pushing out a poop, they'd scoop him up and set him on the toilet. As he sat on the toilet, they would encourage him to go. He would sit there for the longest time, without pooping into the toilet. As soon as he got off, he filled his pants. Believing James' behavior was defiant, his parents became emotional and pleaded with him to change. "You pooped in your pants again? Why do you keep doing this? It's such a mess. You're too big for this. It's disgusting. I can't stand cleaning up these dirty pants any longer."

—continued on next page

His parents viewed James' pooping in his underwear right after a potty-sitting session as evidence of remarkable control. However, when upset or under stress, some children are *unable* to relax the muscles to let the poop out. This was likely the case with James.

It's easy to see that emotions run high in power struggles. It may be that James couldn't resist the personal power he felt in being able to send his parents into a rage. If so, it was just response from Josh and Allyson that kept the power struggle going.

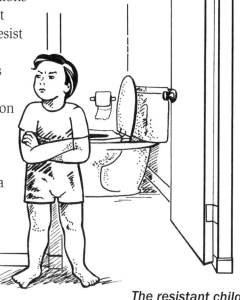

On the surface, an angry parental stance might appear a viable technique to promote toilet training. After all, don't children want to please their parents and avoid angry outbursts? Most children do, but not all. James'

The resistant child

story illustrates how a negative interaction can become a new, daily routine.

—continued from previous page

The family's negative routine compounded the problem. It went like this: Mom and Dad would develop a new plan to persuade James to poop in the toilet. No matter what, he refused to comply and pooped his pants. Mom and Dad became mad and frustrated and James cried. Then Mom and Dad shrugged their shoulders and threw up their hands. Lastly, one parent cleaned him up, all the while pleading with him and trying to convince him of the importance of pooping in the toilet. This routine—even though unpleasant—brought consistency to James' day.

Children may continually pull their parents back into old ways of behaving—even negative ways—because those routines make life predictable. Changing such a routine is difficult, but not impossible.

Remember, a key factor contributing to the problem in the example above is that James received lots of attention for the negative bowel movement routine. Too much of the parent-child interaction revolved around James' bowel habits. To end the battle, his parents needed to change the focus of their relationship with their son.

RESPONDING TO POWER STRUGGLES

To end a power struggle, parents need a plan and a matter-of-fact attitude. Sometimes parents resolve a problem by holding onto their power and control; this is essential when the issue concerns a child's safety—such as wearing a seat belt. In other situations, agreement between parent and child can be reached by offering the child a choice. For example, if Dad is battling with his daughter over getting dressed, offering her a choice about what to wear often resolves the problem. Choices provide children with a measure of control and often defuse a power struggle.

When parents try to exert control in an area where they have none, like bowel and bladder habits, a power struggle usually results. In potty training, it is appropriate for a parent to drop out of such a power struggle. Parents have lots of influence when it comes to teaching their child to use the toilet, but if the learning stops and an emotional battle erupts, parents must drop back. Josh and Allyson from the example above, unfortunately, didn't do this. They believed they could eventually convince their son to poop in the toilet. They thought they could figure out a technique to control what was going on inside his body and mind.

They made endless attempts to convince James to cooperate. They would talk and talk to James about the importance of using the toilet and about how easy life would be if only he would change his bowel habits. They would ask him why he kept pooping his pants? They would even ask him how he planned to go through life if he never pooped in the toilet? Like many parents, they somehow believed they'd be able to convince their son how easy and important it was to go in the toilet and he would agree and cooperate. An outcome like this was highly unlikely.

To end such a contest of wills, parents need to admit they have lost the battle. When they come to this realization, they must drop out of the conflict and turn control completely over to their child. It is paradoxical, but when parents stop trying to control a child, he or she is likely to begin to use the toilet.

STEPS TO END A POTTY TRAINING POWER STRUGGLE

Sometimes problems between parent and child involve bowel training, sometimes urine training, and sometimes both. Whatever the extent of the problem, the remedy is similar. The following is a bowel training example, but you can easily adapt the approach to a urine training struggle as well.

Step 1: Give Control to the Child

Say, "You get to decide where to poop. Someday you'll feel ready to poop in the toilet. It's okay with me if you want to poop in your underwear (or diaper) for now."

Step 2: Stay Calm or Pretend to Stay Calm

When the child poops her pants, take her to the bathroom and clean her up. It's important to be totally matter-of-fact in your body language and voice inflec-

> ### Change Wet or Poopy Pants Promptly
>
> Don't leave children in wet or poopy diapers or underwear. Some parents believe if they prolong the wet or messy sensations, the child will be motivated to use the toilet. However, it is more effective, humane, and sanitary to change the child in a timely fashion so she becomes accustomed to dry and clean undergarments. It also avoids the rashes or yeast infections caused by unchanged diapers.

tion. Do not sigh, look disgusted, annoyed, or angry. Try not to establish eye contact as you clean your child; don't talk, just clean her up as quickly as possible and then move on through the day.

Step 3: Pretend You Don't Care

Do not look for signs of when your child is about to poop. In fact, if you notice she is pooping her pants, slowly walk away. You don't want to give your child any attention when she is pooping in her underwear. Don't talk about bowel training in front of her. Don't hint or make any suggestions about using the toilet. If you are really bothered by accidents, go back to diapers for a while.

Step 4: Stay Connected in Other Ways

Establish a relationship with your child totally separate from bowel training. (See page 33 in Chapter 2 for suggestions.)

Step 5: Involve your Child in the Cleanup Process

Use the above new approach for a week or so. Then if the child is about three and a half or older (and able to do so), inform her that she needs to clean *herself* up after she has a bowel movement in her underwear. Escort her to the bathroom and put her in the bathtub. Coach her through each step of the cleanup process, being completely nonchalant in your body language and voice inflection. You need to encourage her, being friendly and kind, but it's important to remain firm about her cleaning herself up as much as she is able. Children younger than two and a half years cannot manage this task on their own. Whatever age the child is, in the end, it's important for you to check that she is clean and, if necessary, finish up the final wipes yourself.

Your goal is to teach your child the natural consequence for pooping in her pants is cleaning herself up. It's okay if your child expresses some frustration here, but be careful not to send the message that this is a punishment.

Step 6: Sympathize with the Difficulty of Cleaning up

If your child gets emotional, you can sympathize, "I know it's hard work cleaning up poopy pants. You don't like doing it." Then set the limit again, "Nevertheless, when you poop in your underwear, you have to clean it up. I'll help get your shoes and socks off." You may be tempted to say, "If you'd poop in the toilet, you wouldn't have this mess to deal with." But it's best not to make this comment. Instead, phrase it positively, "Someday you'll poop in the toilet. Then you won't need to clean all this up."

Step 7: Find Other Children to Model the Process

It's a good idea to invite a young cousin, neighbor, or friend over to play who is skilled in using the toilet. Be sure to ask her parents if your child can go in the bathroom with their child so she can see how the other child manages pooping in the toilet. Also, ask your young visitor for permission. Be careful how involved you get in staging this event. The more naturally it occurs, the better.

Another option is to put your child in a quality child care setting a couple days a week so she can see the ease with which other children poop in the toilet. Watching other children in this new environment, with trained teachers to help, might inspire your child to use the toilet for pooping too. Having other children around to demonstrate puts the activity in your child's realm of possibility.

The goal is for your child to discover that pooping in the toilet is much easier than cleaning up messy underpants. Realize that this is something your child must learn in her own way and time.

Step 8: Practice Sitting on the Potty

After you and your child have had a week or so to cool off from all the power struggle upset, set two times daily when she is required to sit on the toilet. As suggested in earlier chapters, you can call it something like Poo–Poo Time or Potty Time. Reassure your child she is not required to perform, she only needs to sit on the toilet. In the beginning, she might sit there only a minute or so; but slowly increase the time to five minutes. You can read her a story, she can look at books herself, or she can listen to an audio story.

Sitting still is very difficult for some high energy children. Show them that they can wiggle their fingers or tap their toes while sitting. Some may really not be able to sit for more than two to three minutes. At first, your child can sit on the toilet with her clothes on, but later, encourage her to pull her pants down. These practice sessions help the child become comfortable with sitting on the toilet. Then, when the time is right for her to use it, the experience won't be foreign or scary.

Step 9: Back Off and Wait Until Your Child Is Ready

Now you must step back emotionally and wait until your child finally decides for herself to poop in the toilet. Be patient; you can't hurry the process.

Step 10: If Backing Off Is Hard, Get Support

If you sense yourself growing more and more emotional or out-of-control, call someone for help and ideas—your doctor, a nurse, your mother, a friend, or a parent educator. If you are really worried about your child's health, consult your child's pediatrician or your family doctor first. If your child has unexpected trouble holding urine (which can be a sign of a urinary tract infection) or if she holds her bowel movements in for more than three to five days, definitely call the doctor. You may need to have your child checked out physically to make sure all systems are working properly.

It is very important to distinguish between *won't* use the potty and *can't* use the potty. What looks like intentional defiance can sometimes be *inability*. Check with your pediatrician. Also see Chapter 8: Children with Special Needs.

Step 11: Appreciate Success Without Going Overboard

When your child finally does go in the toilet, show interest, but don't go overboard with praise. A simple response like, "Good for you!" along with a homemade certificate of "Congratulations" to post on the refrigerator, are all that's necessary.

Once you develop a plan to end a power struggle, it's important to stick with it. Wait about three weeks for any significant improvement. Quick fixes seldom occur. Keep in mind the three P's: Persistence, Patience, and a Plan. Remember that changing daily from one plan to another is quite bewildering to children and hinders more than it helps.

PROVIDE A DIAPER FOR POOPS

Many children who are urine trained still request a diaper for their bowel movements. When this happens, parents often feel controlled by their child and respond by refusing the diaper; they plead with their child or pressure him to perform on the toilet instead. The end result is a power struggle. This is a common problem.

It's important to provide the diaper for your child. If you don't, many children (like the one in the story below) will refuse to poop for days, starting on a path of constipation and bowel retention. (See Chapter 10 for more information on this problem.) This is dangerous for a child's body.

If your child requests a diaper for bowel movements well after he is urine trained, try gradually guiding the child toward pooping in the toilet. Remember not to panic; your child will eventually poop there.

Stories from the Bathroom

No Diaper, No Poop *(Jamahl, almost 4 years)*

Darla's son, Jamahl, insisted on wearing a diaper for his bowel movements. He had been urine trained for over a year, but would not poop in the toilet. Darla tried every trick in the book. She told him she'd take him to the toy store and buy him anything he wanted if he'd poop in the toilet just once. It did no good. She yelled, restricted, pleaded, reasoned, and even spanked, but nothing coerced him to perform on the toilet.

So when the current box of diapers ran out, Darla informed him that she was not going to buy any more. She thought that if he didn't have diapers, he'd be forced to go in the toilet. Jamahl retained his bowel movement for four days. Wisely, Darla bought diapers again. Jamahl went back to the old "I need a diaper" routine. Off he went to his bedroom to poop and then Darla cleaned him up.

After giving it some thought, Darla came up with the following plan. One day she said to her son, "Jamahl, it's your body. If you need a diaper the rest of your life, I will see that you have one and I will love you just the same. But once you get your diaper on, I'd like you to go into the bathroom to poop. That way you won't smell up your bedroom and it's easier for me to clean you up in there." Jamahl agreed.

After a few days of pooping in his diaper in the bathroom, Darla requested, "Jamahl, now when I put a

—continued on next page

—continued from previous page

diaper on, I'd like you to sit on the toilet." At first, he had trouble pushing a poop out as he sat on the toilet with his diaper on. It was difficult to change positions from squatting to sitting; using a small footstool helped. In time, with encouragement from his mom, he adjusted to sitting on the toilet with the diaper still in place.

Darla also established a practice time when Jamahl was required to sit on the toilet twice a day, underwear off, for a brief amount of time, to rehearse pooping in the toilet. Darla assured Jamahl he was not expected to go, he just needed to sit there.

As he sat on the toilet to practice, Darla told him a made-up story about a little boy who didn't know how to poop in the toilet. The story included parts about the boy practicing sitting on the toilet, but ending up going in his diaper. The story ended with the boy figuring out one day how to relax his muscles and to go in the toilet and how proud the boy felt when he finally accomplished this task. Jamahl enjoyed the story. If Darla left out or changed even one part, he corrected her.

Finally one day, out of the blue, as Jamahl was sitting on the toilet with his diaper in place, he said, "You can take my diaper off, Mom," and that was the end of it. He pooped in the toilet. This process took two weeks.

So what's to be learned from the stories of James and Jamahl? First, children are in control of their bowels and bladders. There is no way to force a child to go in the toilet. In fact, if you get into an emotional power struggle, children will often delay instead of progressing steadily on their own potty-learning timeline. Performing on the toilet is your child's decision, not yours.

WHY PARENTS MAY GET INTO POWER STRUGGLES

Expecting a child to use the toilet seems reasonable enough. When a generally reasonable request meets resistance, parents sometimes overreact—it's hard to understand why the child balks. Plus, parents have been changing diapers for years and just want to be done. Sometimes we wish our children would make life easier for us. Parenting is hard work. At other times parents are unsure about what is really going on. Is it that Jonathan *cannot* manage toileting or *will not?* Parents may mistakenly believe that the child is developmentally ready, when that is not the case. This is especially likely in the case of emotional readiness. A child may be able to use the potty sometimes, but still not be emotionally ready to take on the job all day, every day.

Here's an adult comparison. If we find a person hard to get along with, we can make a special effort to do so for brief or special occasions, but to deal with that person all day, *every* day, would take more emotional energy than we have available. For a child, initially making the effort to get to the potty on time all day long, day after day, can take a *lot* of emotional energy.

Sometimes parents push too hard because they fear training will never happen if they simply wait. In fact, almost *all* children are potty trained by kindergarten and most much earlier. Remember when you held your tiny baby? It seemed impossible that this helpless creature would someday walk. And yet, she did. Development happens.

Some parents have trouble seeing their child as a separate person; they believe they can exert control over the child's bowel and bladder habits. There is a lot a parent can do to influence toileting success, but ultimately, control lies with the child. Just as parents can't force a child to eat or sleep, they can't force a child to use the toilet. When you become too enmeshed in your child's feelings, behaviors, and attitudes, problems occur. This is true whether you're encouraging your child to learn to use the toilet or helping her to improve her reading ability. It's important to keep in mind the boundaries of your control and influence.

PERSONALITY TYPES PRONE TO POWER STRUGGLES

There seems to be a similarity among parents who engage in potty training power struggles with their children. Such parents tend to be highly involved in many aspects of parenting. They like to choose the child's clothes, activities, food, friends, and are often strict disciplinarians.

Parents who are prone to power struggles frequently make the mistake of insisting on mature behavior long before the child is ready. If they demand a child walk a narrow path of acceptable behavior and punish harshly when the child strays from that path, the child unconsciously feels that the only thing in her life she can control are her bowels and bladder and goes overboard to prove this.

So check yourself out. Can you lighten up? Can you alter your expectations regarding your child's behavior? Try asking yourself each time you make a decision for your child, Is this a decision my child could be making for herself? If the answer is yes, back off and let her make it. This will give your child control in positive and appropriate areas of her life, and it won't be as important for her to hold onto those bowel movements.

Stories from the Bathroom

Getting Help *(Roberto, 3 years)*

A potty training power struggle was well underway among Roberto and his parents, Marisol and Julio. Roberto refused to poop in the toilet. His mom and dad would force him to sit on the toilet; they would hold him there because they knew he needed to empty his bowel. Instead of pooping in the toilet or messing his underwear, Roberto began to retain his bowel movements for days. Marisol was a nurse and knew this was unhealthy for his body. Roberto would finally go when Mom or Dad would allow him to wear a diaper to poop, but this was only after angry demands to go in the toilet.

Both Julio and Marisol were enmeshed on a deep emotional level with Roberto in the bowel training issue. They had a hard time seeing Roberto as a separate person who was in control of his bodily functions. They knew they needed to rein in their emotions, but they just couldn't. Roberto's bowel activity was dominating not only their relationship with their son, but their relationship with each other. Red flags were flying all over the place.

Marisol called Roberto's pediatrician, who referred her to a psychologist specializing in play therapy. Once the sessions between Roberto and the therapist began, Marisol and Julio relaxed. Roberto was getting the help he needed, so they felt able to drop out of the power struggle. Within weeks, Roberto was pooping in the toilet.

If your child is resistant to all attempts to toilet train, or if you feel your child is suffering emotionally or psychologically, consider getting a referral from your child's doctor or nurse to see a therapist specializing in children. Sometimes it takes a trained therapist to help a child overcome resistance to toileting. Also, you will feel relief when the burden of training is lifted from your shoulders to those of a skilled professional.

SETTING A LIMIT

In general, the way to avoid power struggles is to back off. However, some situations also require setting limits. See how Marco's mom, in the anecdote below, combined backing off (in terms of using the potty) with setting a firm limit.

Stories from the Bathroom

Diapers Required *(Marco, 3 years)*

   Marco's mom was very relaxed about toilet training. She waited patiently for readiness and didn't assume he'd be interested early on. One day, just after his third birthday, Marco learned how to pull his diapers off. Mom was delighted. She thought Marco was ready for potty training, so she bought training pants. Marco immediately pulled those off as well and peed wherever he was—on the rug, on the couch, anywhere. Mom felt frustrated and helpless for several days until she decided on a plan.

   In order to avoid a power struggle, she put him back in diapers. But to stop him from pulling those diapers down and peeing wherever he was, she put his overalls on backwards so he couldn't get them off. She really had to fight to get them on each time, but felt it was much better than being worried and angry all day about where Marco was going to pee next. After a month, Mom asked Marco if he wanted to wear underwear and pee in the potty. He said, "Yes." She tried training pants again and this time he used the potty.

In general, children respond positively to healthy limits. Marco's mom wasn't trying to force him to pee in the toilet (she provided a diaper), but she was very firm in teaching him that he couldn't pee anywhere he liked.

A Final Word

If you are embroiled in a power struggle with your child over toileting, don't despair. Use the steps in this chapter to gradually step out of this negative cycle. Get support for yourself if necessary. The detached perspective of a professional can help you find peace of mind and do what is best for your child.

7

Working with Child Care Providers

Like parents, child care providers have different ideas about toilet training, depending on the situation and their past experience. When caring for only a few children, providers can more easily see the body wiggles that suggest a need to use the toilet and assist accordingly. In larger groups, some providers include regular potty breaks as part of the daily routine. In other situations, children need to be able to directly indicate their needs to the provider in order to get assistance.

In years past, parents often received inappropriate pressure from grandparents about toilet training. Now, pressure more often comes from preschools that will not admit three year olds unless they are trained. Be realistic about your child's progress and don't get in a power struggle with your child due to someone else's rules. If need be, look for a different child care situation rather than pushing your child toward a goal he cannot meet.

PRESCHOOLS THAT REQUIRE A CHILD BE TRAINED BY AGE THREE

Preschools that insist all children be trained by age three may lack a basic understanding about variation in child development. If this school is misinformed on this topic, do you want to trust it on others? Some schools say the issue is the extra staffing needed to change diapers. It may be that it is simply a business decision. But if staffing is so tight they can't change diapers for the few three year olds who need it, will there be enough staffing to give your child personal attention in other important areas?

You may decide to lean on the staff with a note from your child's doctor. Or, if your child has special needs, you can mention the legal requirement to accommodate him or her. (For more about special needs, see Chapter 8.) However, making a big fuss sometimes only inspires resentment toward your child. It is often better not to try to change the center's policy and simply look for other care. Many parents find that small home child care arrangements are more adaptable than child care centers. Remember that during these early years, a responsive, involved caregiver is more important than cutting-edge facilities and fancy equipment.

One final note, if you have your eye on a center that requires training by age three: it often is not possible to guess ahead of time whether or not your two year old will train by that point. You'll have more peace of mind if you keep two child care options open—one that doesn't require training and one that does—as long as possible.

POINTERS FOR TRAINING WHILE IN CHILD CARE

In working with your child care provider, there are three areas in which to pay attention.

Communication

Many child care providers have a toilet training policy. Read it. Talk with your provider. Although you know your individual child better than anyone else, your provider likely has a lot more experience with toilet training. What is her usual approach? Does she think your child is ready? Does she think her method will be appropriate for your child? If you have different potty training ideas, stay open-minded and discuss these differences. Be sure to relay the exact potty words you use in your family.

Don't conference at the door. If your child is listening, he may misunderstand parts of your conversation. Call your provider when the children are napping, in the evening, or on the weekend. If necessary, set up an appointment. During the training process, talk regularly about successes and setbacks.

When training within the family, children commonly observe parents using the toilet. In child care, issues of safety and privacy arise. When providers work alone and need their own potty breaks, will children join them in the bathroom or be safe alone by themselves? Work out what is comfortable and appropriate for all.

Cooperation

If your provider initiates the training, or if your child shows interest at the center because all of the other kids use the potty, go along with her suggestions and approach. Follow through at home with a similar program. Consistency in both places will help your child progress faster. If the child gets support and encouragement during the week at child care, but not at home on weekends, the process will take longer. Do what you can to support your caregiver through the potty training process.

Consideration

Potty training can be hard for providers who care for children of different ages. If your child has lots of accidents in the child care setting, be sure to provide lots of underpants (or training pants) and easy clothes with elastic waistbands (no snaps, buckles, or zippers). You might need to do laundry daily. Purchase a potty seat for your child to use at child care if your provider doesn't have one.

WHEN VIEWPOINTS DIFFER

What approach should you take if you and your provider see things differently? Do you follow her plan or ask her to follow yours? Ask about her philosophy and experience with toilet training. If she advocates beginning training at a different time than you propose, find out why. As pointed out above, you know your child best. However, her experience with children may bring some new perspective to the table. Be open to her knowledge and opinions. You will be able to discern if the center's approach is in your child's best interests or in its own.

If your provider is new in the field, you may have read more about potty training than she has. Your child's caregiver needs to understand individual differences in development and temperament and know your child well.

Attitude can be more important than a particular time to start. There's no harm in moving ahead sooner than you might have considered, as long as the approach is gentle, respectful, and responsive. Alternatively, if your provider suggests a return to diapers, find out why. Is it because she senses your child is feeling pressured? Is it because she's unsure how to comfortably manage accidents or is it something else entirely? Think and talk through the possibilities and decide how to proceed. You can always change course again, if need be.

It is important to stay calm and remember that you are both on the same team and have the same goal: a child who toilet trains at his best time developmentally. If you cannot agree on an approach, or if your child doesn't respond well to your provider's methods, then it is time to find another child care situation.

Stories from the Bathroom

Mom Gets a Surprise (Olivia, 2 years)

Although Olivia's mom bought a potty chair, she had read that girls, on average, train around two and a half. Mom had decided to wait until then to introduce potty training. She was surprised when her child care provider said, "Please bring training pants and extra clothes on Monday. Olivia watches the other kids and seems interested in the potty." Mom did as she was asked, but because she didn't want to pressure Olivia, she continued to use diapers at home. Over the next several weeks, the provider reported that Olivia was making good progress. Then one Saturday morning, when Mom started to put on a diaper, Olivia protested and pointed to the training pants. Mom put them on

—continued on next page

—continued from previous page

and was amazed that Olivia went through the entire weekend with only one accident.

Problematic Pressure *(Mercedes, 18 months)*

Mom enrolled Mercedes in her current child care at one year. After six months, she was surprised when the provider told her she trains all "her children" at 18 months. Mom thought, "Well, she has more experience. Great, let her do it." As instructed, Mom bought a potty chair for home use and brought training pants and extra clothes to child care. After some weeks, Mom observed she was still bringing home a bag full of wet clothes each day. She also noticed that whenever the home potty caught Mercedes' attention, she got very quiet and looked sad. Mom couldn't get many details out of the provider about how training was going, but it looked like pain and shame on Mercedes' face. Mom decided to find new child care immediately.

USES THE POTTY AT PRESCHOOL, BUT NOT AT HOME

Some parents report that their child uses the potty at preschool, but refuses to do so at home. Remember that because children are more closely attached to parents, they struggle more to demonstrate their independence from us. Get details from your provider about what works there and gently do the same at home without pressure or power struggles.

Try not to get too upset. Eventually, your child will be toilet trained in all settings. Be glad she's progressing in at least one venue.

In general, being in child care offers many opportunities for your child to see other children his or her age using the bathroom regularly. It puts toileting in their realm of possibility and provides positive role-modeling. Just be wary of pressuring your child to train in order to be admitted to a preschool program; no school deadline is worth a potty-training power struggle. You want your child to train on the timetable that is right for him.

8

Children with Special Needs—Visible and Invisible

Families of children with disabilities or other special needs have many of the very same toilet training issues as all other children. Thus, all the other chapters of this book are relevant as well. This chapter contains specific information pertaining to special-needs potty training and will answer some common questions parents have.

WILL MY CHILD BECOME ABLE TO MANAGE INDEPENDENTLY? WHEN?

The good news is that 95% of children with special needs eventually do learn to manage toileting on their own. Many will need more time than other children; age five or even later is not uncommon. However, with the many differences in ordinary development and temperament, plus the wide array of special needs, there is no standard timetable.

The best course of action is to talk with the professionals who know your child—pediatrician, nurse practitioner, physical therapist, occupational therapist, education specialists, and perhaps others. They will have the specialized knowledge and experience to advise you on what kind of timetable is likely. Look for children several years older than your child with similar disabilities. Ask their parents when they trained and what tips they might have to offer you. Because of individual variation, the more people you ask, the more likely you are to find helpful ideas and advice that meet your needs. Helper ingenuity is another significant influence on when special-needs children learn the steps of toileting.

WHAT ARE YOUR CHILD'S SPECIFIC ISSUES?

Take a moment to look at the big picture. Take into account what you know from your health care providers and what you know about other children with special needs and rate your child in each of the following areas on the chart below. Those with mild symptoms may need extra time and help or may turn out to be very similar to children in general. At the moderate level, children will need more time, assistance, and creativity in order to reach toileting independence. Even with severe involvement, many will become independent. A small number will continue to need assistance with some aspects of toileting.

Type of Special Need	Effects on Potty Training	Mild	Moderate	Severe
Learning issues: Difficulty in expressing wants/needs or in understanding others. Examples are mild cognitive impairment, learning disabilities, sometimes autism, Down syndrome, and pervasive developmental delay (PDD)	Children may have difficulty understanding why they need to use the toilet; they may have difficulty expressing the need to go; and it may be hard for them to understand how to use the toilet and perform hygiene tasks. The learning process will probably take extra time.			
Sensory issues: Difficulty taking in information. This includes hearing and vision problems. Some children get very little sensation from skin, bowels, or bladder. Others (including some cases of autism) get strong or overwhelming sensations.	Issues are as varied as the ability to find an unfamiliar toilet, aiming into the toilet (for boys), noticing wetness, feeling the need to go, or being overwhelmed by the sound of a flushing toilet.			

Type of Special Need	Effects on Potty Training	Mild	Moderate	Severe
Muscle issues: May affect strength, mobility, or ability to relax once on the toilet. Examples include cerebral palsy, muscular dystrophy, and spinal cord injury.	The effort involved in getting on and off the toilet is probably the biggest issue here. May also have difficulty dressing, wiping, flushing, or washing hands.			

When children have obvious special needs, most adults understand that extra time and patience will be needed for toilet training. However, some children, who have no obvious disabilities, may still have special needs as far as potty training is concerned—see the story of Madison below. Unfortunately, adults may mistakenly believe that these children are being defiant rather than simply needing help.

Stories from the Bathroom

Low Awareness of Body Signals *(Madison, almost 5 years)*

Madison would be attending kindergarten in the fall. She was bowel trained but still peed her pants two or three times a day. When her mom, Rebecca, picked her up from preschool, Madison would be involved in play and totally wet. She wasn't bothered by her soaked clothes.

As Rebecca tried to solve this urinating puzzle, she changed tactics almost weekly. One week, she'd try rewarding Madison with a new toy for peeing in the toilet, but when Madison had an accident, she'd lose control and yell or reprimand. The next week, she tried to completely ignore the wet pants, but by the second accident, Rebecca found herself tense and angry. The following week, she

—continued on next page

—continued from previous page

would remind Madison every hour to sit on the toilet; often she had no success. Changing approaches so often was very confusing for Madison.

Rebecca wondered what would happen next year in kindergarten. What if wetting her pants continued into the first grade? Rebecca also worried how friends and family were judging Madison. She saw the raised eyebrows and head shaking. What exasperated Rebecca most was that the wet pants didn't seem to bother Madison at all. If she could see that Madison was upset about the soaked panties, or was at least trying to make it to the toilet, she would feel more hopeful and more patient.

Finally, Rebecca decided to consult Madison's pediatrician. The doctor surmised that Madison received little sensation from her bladder about the need to go. Some children feel this sensation loud and clear, but not Madison. The result was that she required more maturing time than most children to read the signal from her body and know when it was time to find a toilet.

Dad didn't really believe what the doctor told Rebecca. He wanted to spank Madison each time she peed in her pants. He was convinced if Madison knew she'd get a spanking, she'd start using the toilet to avoid the punishment.

Rebecca took Dad with her to the next doctor appointment. The pediatrician advised them to view Madison's problem as a delay in development. If a specialist told them that Madison wouldn't be able to walk until some time between five and six years old, they wouldn't yell or

Spanking Not Advised
Spanking is never appropriate when guiding a child toward learning to use the toilet. In fact, swats on the bottom actually delay the process. Anxiety can make it harder to relax and let go when on the toilet. In addition, pain and humiliation build resentment toward parents. All of these effects hinder training.

—continued on next page

—continued from previous page

spank to force her across the room. They would be patient, explain the problem to family and friends, and provide assistance as Madison struggled to learn to walk. The pediatrician recommended they set aside their emotions and develop a plan. He advised sticking with it as long as necessary for Madison to achieve success.

Rebecca explained the situation to Madison, "The doctor says your body is a little different. Many children feel the need to pee clearly; it's almost like a fire engine's siren telling them it's time to run to the bathroom and go in the toilet. Your body doesn't give out loud signals—your body gives out quiet signals, so you need to listen harder. Right now, sometimes you hear it and sometimes you don't. After a while, you'll hear it every single time."

Rebecca observed Madison carefully. She noticed that, at home, Madison seldom experienced urinating mishaps. At preschool, or when playing at friends' houses, the accidents occurred more often. Although she could remind Madison to use the toilet every hour at home, she wanted to put the ball in Madison's court—let her learn from the consequence of having to change wet clothes herself.

Here's the plan Rebecca decided on. At home, she would let Madison change her own wet clothes to help her notice the problem. To avoid the negative attention from others when her clothes were wet in public, Mom put her in cloth training pants covered by thin plastic pants. She sent along extra dry clothing with her to school. Madison responded well to this program. She rarely had accidents in kindergarten and by first grade was in regular panties at school.

MEDICATIONS YOUR CHILD MAY TAKE

Bladder and bowel function requires the use of both voluntary and involuntary muscles. (Voluntary muscles act when we decide to do something such as lift a glass of water. Involuntary muscles work without our thinking about them—such as mixing the food in our stomachs.) A variety of medicines or their side effects can tighten or relax these two types of muscles—so they may affect toileting. Given this complexity, ask your doctor if any medicines your child takes may impact the training process.

With certain disabilities, medications are essential for toileting. For example, with spinal cord problems, intestinal muscles or abdominal muscles (which normally help push) may not contract strongly enough to push out stool. Or, muscles at the opening of the rectum may be too tight or too loose. Bowel medicines can help with such difficulties. Here too, work closely with your child's doctor.

EMOTIONAL CHALLENGES FOR FAMILIES WITH SPECIAL NEEDS

Confusion and anxiety are common in families facing toilet training a child with special needs. It's painful to see one's child on a different track from what you expected and hoped. When children lag in reaching developmental milestones and it becomes apparent they will likely continue to lag, parents often feel overwhelmed at the prospect of having to provide certain types of care for much longer than they had initially imagined.

Some parents are tossed among the opposing winds of denial and despair. Others frantically try to push delayed children to keep up with their age mates. Still other parents, overwhelmed with the added care, extra medical appointments, and so forth, avoid the entire issue of toilet training for months or even years longer than necessary because diapers are familiar and seem easier than training.

On the other hand, if independent toileting is really not possible for your child, it is important to set this issue aside and instead, focus on building success in other areas.

YOUR INDIVIDUAL PLAN

Given the variation among all children to begin with, plus variations in both types and severity of special needs, a one-size potty-training plan definitely does not fit all. Your plan will be very individual. Closely observe your child. A realistic appraisal of his capabilities is essential. Combine everything you know about your child and everything you learn from knowledgeable experts and other parents. Put it together to come up with a good plan for *your* child. The patterns you set now will have long-term effects. The goal is to teach a toileting method this child will be able to use in the long run with as much independence as possible. The more information and skill children develop in *this* life skill, the better equipped they will be to handle future tasks.

With special needs, learning to use the toilet will likely take more time and energy than in other families. However, don't limit your child's future options and independence because the task seems overwhelming to you right now. Where do you hope to see your child in three to five years? When the time is right, what small step can you take in that direction? Clearly observe and note what your child can do by herself and with what steps she needs help.

Once you are ready, you need your child on board as well. A straightforward approach is to say, "You want to be like other kids and go to bathroom by yourself.[7] This is what you need to do to get there." Invite your child's input and ideas. Just thinking through the process is practice for other issues that are bound to come along. Encourage your child to be in charge of as much as possible and to manage independently as much as he can.

Be creative in selecting methods that realistically work for your particular child and family. As one mother said, "Disability teaches you creativity." One mom provided a creative incentive by telling her four-year-old daughter, "If you get yourself to the toilet after you get up in the morning, you can pick out your clothes for the day. Otherwise, I'll pick your clothes." Her daughter, who dearly loved to pick out her own outfits, responded well to this incentive.

SHORTCUTS CAN UNDERMINE HEALTH

Be careful about "shortcuts" that can be hazardous to your child's health. Pressure to hold urine for long periods or excessive fluid restriction may seem useful in short run, but can cause long-term harm. For more information, see Dangerous Shortcuts, page 72, in Chapter 5, and information on daily liquid needs, pages 45–46, in Chapter 3.

---

[7] Assuming your child is realistically able to accomplish potty training.

You might also hear about the ease of indwelling catheters—a plastic tube that drains urine from the bladder into an outside plastic bag. Indwelling catheters can seem an easy solution, but they increase the risk of infection and may, with years of use, increase the risk of bladder cancer. Although some physical disabilities require the use of laxatives to maintain a healthy bowel schedule, most do not. Your child's doctor should *always* be involved with any decision to use laxatives. Talk with knowledgeable health professionals about what is best for your child over the long haul.

WHEN SHOULD I START TRAINING MY SPECIAL-NEEDS CHILD?

In general, begin at the same time that other age mates are starting. This provides examples to follow and incentive to join in the activity. As you start the process, think about how your child best learns other skills and use the same approaches to toileting. (Another possible option is the very early training method for infants discussed in Chapter 11. This method has been used successfully with various disabilities, including Down syndrome, autism, and blindness.)

Stories from the Bathroom

Nicholas with pervasive developmental delay
(PDD) (2 to 5 years)

Sonia tried to get Nicholas to sit on the potty chair at home when the other two year olds in child care began training. He refused the little potty chair but was willing to sit on the regular toilet. This was fine with his mom and dad. He loved being with his dad and liked to copy him in the bathroom. Although he occasionally had success, he still wore diapers most of the time.

When he was about three and a half, Sonia decided the real time had come. She put underwear on him and took him to the bathroom after meals, before going out, and whenever they arrived at their destination.

—continued on next page

—continued from previous page

He got used to being dry and liked it. His bowel schedule had always been pretty regular, so Sonia was able to have him in the bathroom at those times. In the evening, she reduced his fluids slightly. She usually took him to the bathroom once during the night. In kindergarten, he still had occasional accidents, but after that, almost never.

Lamont with developmental delay *(3 years)*

Lamont's mother, Kareema, realized that after years of highly absorbent diapers, she had no idea how often her son needed to pee. One week when she was home in the summer, she decided that he was ready to potty train. She stayed outside with him, left off his diaper, and gave him lots of liquids. She observed his body signals and patterns of urinating. Then she set a potty schedule accordingly. She assumed, correctly, that because of his developmental delay, he would need extra time to completely train. In order to keep it simple, she always followed the same steps, in the same order, and told all his various caregivers (babysitters, grandparents, preschool teachers) what words they used at home for potty training.

Michael with autism *(2½ to 4½ years)*

Kate knew early on that something was developmentally amiss with their son Michael, but nothing was clear enough to diagnose. They tried training him when he was between two and three, but he refused to sit on the potty. He cried and Kate yelled. When she took the diaper off, he simply wouldn't go. He'd wait until she put him back in a diaper for naptime or bedtime, and then pee. The pediatrician told Mom to back off—he assured her that Michael would eventually use the potty. They put him back in diapers and found an accepting preschool.

At four, he was diagnosed with autism. Once Kate learned that strong opinions about where things belonged were part of autism, she understood what interfered with the potty training. It was Michael's opinion that pee and poop belonged in a diaper.

—continued on next page

—continued from previous page

Later, Michael observed his younger sister go from diapers, to potty chair, to toilet—winning her "potty prizes" along the way. He watched with interest. Kate bought two fancy toy trucks. She told Michael he could have them when he was willing to use the potty chair. The trucks waited in sight on high shelves—one at home and one at preschool. Still, he showed no inclination to make any changes.

As Michael approached four and a half, Kate decided it was time for further measures. On a day she was home, she took off his diaper, set the potty chair nearby, started his favorite program on TV, and kept offering him lots of juice. She knew he wouldn't pee on the floor, so the potty was his only option. That was the day he earned the truck at home. He returned to preschool in diapers, but within a few days, came home with the other truck. Both of these days were turning points in his potty training journey.

Mom also rewarded each significant step after that—changing to the toilet, standing up to pee—with little Hot Wheels® cars. Rewards were the key in his potty training success. Mom hit on the special item (toy vehicles) that motivated Michael. Candy or other incentives did not work for him.

HELPFUL AIDS AND EQUIPMENT

Check your local drug, hardware, discount store, or even camping supply store for adaptive toilet seats, grab bars, and other useful products. Equipment in medical supply stores can sometimes be unnecessarily expensive. Look for things that are easy to use and convenient for the rest of the family. Disposable diapers come in all sizes, including 40-100 pounds. You may have to check labels carefully to find them. The absorption capacity of the typical disposable diaper can be extended by inserting a washable cotton pad inside the diaper for long trips, outings, or impractical settings.

Aids for Communication and Memory

If your child isn't talking yet, make up hand signals for "wet", "dry", "poopy", and "need to use the potty." Put pictures of the following steps beside the toilet:

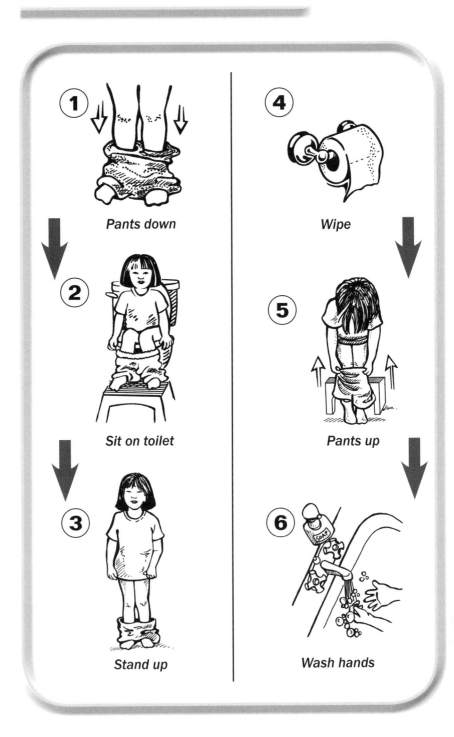

1. Pants down
2. Sit on toilet
3. Stand up
4. Wipe
5. Pants up
6. Wash hands

Or use an inexpensive voice recorder on a neck-band to provide step-by-step instructions at the push of a button. Such reminders help reinforce the sequence and can help the child focus on the task at hand. Keeping track of your child's urinating and elimination patterns may also help; if you know when she needs to go, you can arrange to be on hand.

Aids for Sensory Issues

A clock is likely to be your best tool early on. In other words, keep a clear record of what times of day your child pees and poops for at least one week. If you can determine her patterns, you can make some reasonable decisions on the best times to take her to the toilet. Most children benefit from a regular schedule of potty breaks every two to three hours during the day. Watch-like timers that vibrate at set times can serve as a reminder for older children to use the toilet. Boys who are blind may sit to urinate or stand against the toilet and listen carefully to ensure good aim.

Aids for Mobility Issues

Whenever possible, plan ahead so there is plenty of time to manage getting on and off the toilet comfortably. Extra time is often needed to change positions and place equipment. Dress children in easy-to-manage clothes; use Velcro® instead of snaps, zippers, or buttons. Instead of overalls, use pants with elastic waistbands that are easy to pull down and up. Keeko (more about her later), who uses a wheelchair due to cerebral palsy, was seven and wanted to manage on her own at school. So she skipped underpants altogether. Mom folded two towels onto the bottom of the wheelchair seat each morning. Keeko could remove the top one if it got wet and still have another in place to get through the remainder of the school day.

Look around. Extra support in the bathroom may already be there in the form of a cabinet or sink. Or a potty designed to fit into a corner may give the added support that is needed. Early on, for a young child with severe muscle difficulty, you may be her or his best support. Hold the child on your lap, with a pot between your thighs. Over time, any of the following may be useful: grab bars, portable toilet inserts, wheelchairs with removable arms (or a partially removable bottom), or a board to slide onto the toilet. Boys can easily pee into a container and pour it into the toilet. If there is no accessible toilet available, urine can be inconspicuously transported in a green soda bottle. Some girls in wheelchairs avoid difficult transfers by using a banana-shaped female urinal (available in medical equipment stores and in some camping stores). It takes some planning and skill to get the angle right so urine doesn't spill; practice at home first. If wiping with toilet paper is difficult, a bidet spray may be easier.

For air travel, when getting into the airplane bathroom isn't practical, a diaper can be a lifesaver. Faced with a long airplane flight, one parent of a child with cerebral palsy arranged for the temporary use of an indwelling catheter.

Stories from the Bathroom

Lily with cerebral palsy (3 to 10 years)

Lily had severe cerebral palsy. At three, she had no interest in using the potty. The doctor said not to worry about it yet, but Mom thought it would be easier for her to learn along with the others at her preschool.

Mom felt really alone, trying to figure it all out. She couldn't tell whether Lily's lack of interest was emotional resistance or due to the physical difficulty the disability posed. Mom started looking for adults with similar disabilities and asked them, "I'm trying to help my daughter. What do you remember about toilet training or what have you been told? How do you manage now? Can you help me?"

Given what she learned, Mom decided to put Lily on a standard potty chair at regular intervals. She was fairly successful with urine training. Mom had observed that she shivered just before having a bowel movement in her diaper. Given her unreliable muscle control, Lily needed adaptive equipment to feel physically secure enough to relax on the potty or toilet; she needed support for her arms, a toilet seat insert to give her

—continued on next page

—continued from previous page

trunk more stability, and a belt to hold her in place. Transfer to the toilet took time to learn as well.

Early on, Mom scheduled potty visits every two to three hours. For much of her communication, Lily used an electronic speech board. However, she could also nod Yes and No. So in time, Mom would ask, "Do you need to go?" or "Do you need a change?" and Lily would respond Yes or No. Mom would also say, "Please try to use the bathroom before we go out." Now, at age ten, Lily manages just fine at home. She only needs a diaper when she's out because public toilets just aren't practical for her.

Keeko with cerebral palsy *(3 ½ years to 12 years)*

Keeko has cerebral palsy and uses a wheelchair. Keeko's mom, Carlin, also uses a wheelchair due to polio. Mom knew how important it was to maximize Keeko's bathroom independence. They started training when Keeko was three and a half. Things were going pretty well a year later. To manage by herself, Keeko needed grab bars, which were, of course, available at home. In public bathrooms, transfers to the toilet were easier if she faced one bar, pulled to standing, then sat sideways on the toilet.

To avoid the hard work of transfers, Keeko would sometimes hold her urine. Worried about her health, Mom began to insist on more regular toilet use, "You have to go before you can eat." After she turned five, if Keeko refused to use the toilet before bedtime, and therefore woke Mom for help during the night, Mom charged her a big fee from her allowance. If Keeko used the toilet before bedtime and still needed help during the night, Mom willingly helped for free.

Keeko became independent at home, where the environment was set up for her use. Mom also wanted her to be able to get the help she needed when she was out with other adults. So she taught Keeko how to ask for help and how to explain exactly what she needed to brace the wheelchair between the toilet and the wall, pull up to standing, pants down, turn, and sit.

As Keeko's mom understood, helping children be in charge of the *process* helps them feel more self-confident.

IMPORTANCE OF SUPPORTIVE SCHOOL OR CENTER STAFF

Try to choose child care and schools that have supportive toileting policies and practices. Fortunately, there are many such schools. You can have a friendly meeting with school personnel and set up a plan for toileting. Don't assume the staff will automatically know how to help; you may need to train them. Most public schools have programs for special-needs children where an individual plan is established for each particular child. Make sure that toileting is discussed when you set up this plan.

Some parents have a harder time with establishing toileting help at school. One mother learned that her daughter was holding her urine all day at school because the school personnel refused the help she needed in the bathroom. Another mother, during preschool interviews, learned that all three year olds were expected to use the toilet independently, including wiping, and washing their hands. This mother knew that was unrealistic for her able-bodied son and certainly wouldn't work for her special-needs son.

You have options. Request a meeting to discuss a better toileting plan for your child. If the school's response is not positive, you may be able to motivate their participation with a letter from your child's doctor and mention of the Americans with Disabilities Act (ADA). On the other hand, if your child's toileting needs result in resistance and resentful treatment of your child, looking for another school may be your best course of action.

TAKING ONE STEP AT A TIME

The following checklist breaks the potty training process down into small steps. Some will be easy for your child to master, while others may take planning and creative problem solving. What can your child do now? What can your child learn to do next? What can you do? Who can help? It is not a race, but a pathway toward maximizing independence.

☐ Recognizing the need to go (both pee and poop).
☐ Telling others, I need to go potty.
☐ Asking for help, if necessary, and explaining what is needed.
☐ Getting to the bathroom.
☐ Managing clothes (both off and on).
☐ Getting on and off the potty/toilet.
☐ Using abdominal muscles to push out stool.
☐ Wiping afterward.
☐ Leaving the bathroom tidy for the next person.
☐ Washing and drying hands.

Be pleased and encouraging with each step. All progress toward the child's maximum ability is important and is cause for a pat on the back.

9

Night Training and Bedwetting

Most children learn to stay dry during the night between three and five years of age. Naptime dryness often happens naturally with very little prompting from parents. Children may stop napping or the bladder grows larger and muscles develop enough strength to hold in urine while the child sleeps. Similarly, some children simply start waking in the morning with dry diapers. Others need more help along the way.

Bedwetting[8] is more common in boys and is often an inherited trait; usually children who have difficulty gaining control have one or both parents who had the same problem as a child.

Sleep cycles affect nighttime dryness. Most children pass through about six to eight sleep cycles during the night. These cycles—from light to deep sleep and back to light—last about one and a half hours. Some children are more regular in their sleep cycles than others. The majority of children automatically hold their urine during deep sleep. On the other hand, older children, who wet the bed often, do so when deeply asleep. We will refer back to sleep cycles later in this chapter.

Some parents are reluctant to put a diaper on for sleeping as they fear this gives the child a mixed message. If they've told the child, "No more diapers—only babies use diapers," then why does your big girl or boy need a diaper on for naps? They wonder, what does this

---

[8] The medical term for bedwetting is nocturnal enuresis.

say to the child?

First of all, you can avoid this bind by not equating babies with diapers. Many toddlers wear diapers; some three year olds wear diapers; people with bladder control problems wear diapers; and many older people wear diapers. Some children who use the toilet during the day need a diaper for their nap or through the night.

When your child is using the toilet confidently while awake and questions you as you're putting a diaper on for nap or bedtime, just reassure him or her this way, "Someday you won't need a diaper when you're sleeping. It's best to wear one for now, so your clothes, pajamas, sheets, and blankets don't get wet."

Stories from the Bathroom

Child Knows Best *(Chloe, almost 3 years)*

Chloe had just learned to use the toilet. As Nancy, her mom, put a diaper on her for bed, Chloe protested, "I don't want a diaper, Mom." Nancy didn't want to face wet sheets in the morning or be awakened by Chloe in the middle of the night with a wet bed. But Chloe insisted on pajamas only. Miraculously, Chloe woke up dry the next morning. Staying dry all day and all night happened quickly and easily for Chloe.

Many children, like Chloe, learn to stay dry at night while learning at the same time to use the toilet during the day. Other children gain nighttime control about six months after they regularly use the toilet during the day. Still other children have physical issues that interfere with nighttime training.

HELPFUL STEPS FOR NIGHTTIME TRAINING

When you feel the time is right to work on nighttime training, here are some steps to take.

Make It a Short Trip

Place a potty chair or other container by the bedside. Keep a night light on in the room. This avoids a trip down a long, possibly scary, hallway.

Daytime Attention

Encourage the child to notice and respond to bladder urges when they are first felt during the day. This will help him learn to notice early cues when he is in light stages of sleep at night.

Wake the Child

Some parents *carry* their child to the bathroom to pee before they themselves go to bed each night. This works well in some families while waiting for bladder size to increase. Most children will eventually hold their urine all night long, while others will need to get up at least once a night for the rest of their lives. For this second group, the parents are setting up a pattern the child will need to continue. If the child is too sleepy to wake up and perform, try waking him 30 to 45 minutes earlier or later, to correspond with a lighter stage of sleep. Encourage the child to wake enough to walk to the bathroom. Continuing to use diapers or disposable underpants at night may delay nighttime dryness for these children; they will have no incentive to get up. A wet bed is more noticeable.

CONSIDER DIET

A child's diet can affect nighttime wetting. Cola drinks with caffeine can make the bladder muscle tight so that it holds less urine. Constipation can also contribute to night wetting since there is less space for a full bladder.

Food allergies cause nighttime wetting (and daytime accidents) in a small number of children. The most common foods are milk, wheat, citrus, and chocolate. Is there a family history of allergies? If your child has hay fever, is prone to hives, or has other allergy symptoms, she is more likely to have food sensitivities. If you suspect this may be the case, try eliminating one food at a time from the above list for several weeks. Try the easiest one first, which is likely to be citrus (you may need to eliminate tomatoes along with citrus). Wheat is the hardest to eliminate because it is added to so many foods. Fortunately, many stores now carry wheat-free products. With multiple allergies, you'll have to cut one food, then cut another along with it, and then cut a third food along with the first two. It's hard work, but can really pay off. Check with your doctor, an allergist, a nutritionist, or the Internet for more information.[9]

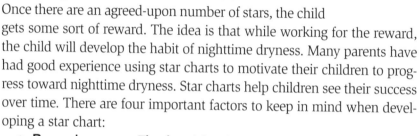

STAR CHARTS

A Star Chart works like this: for every dry night, the child receives a star. Once there are an agreed-upon number of stars, the child gets some sort of reward. The idea is that while working for the reward, the child will develop the habit of nighttime dryness. Many parents have had good experience using star charts to motivate their children to progress toward nighttime dryness. Star charts help children see their success over time. There are four important factors to keep in mind when developing a star chart:

- **Reward success.** The dry nights don't need to occur consecutively. If your child has three dry nights and then wets, it's not fair to take away a star the child has already earned. Subtracting stars is very discouraging; the child just might give up.

- **Be realistic.** Don't make the reward too far in the future. You could start with three dry nights and then give a reward. Then move the goal to six dry nights. This way, your child builds on her successes and gains confidence at the same time. An initial expectation of ten dry nights before a reward will probably defeat the plan.

- **Motivate.** Be certain to choose a reward you know will motivate your child to work toward the goal. For some children, stars alone are enough. For others, a family outing, art supplies, a special snack, or a small toy are more effective. Sometimes the desire for overnights with friends can provide the needed motivation. (For others, whose bodies simply aren't ready yet, you can help them

---

[9] If you're interested in trying an elimination diet, the book, *Is This Your Child? Discovering and Treating Unrecognized Allergies in Children and Adults* by Doris Rapp, M.D., is a good place to start. See the Resource section for more information.

manage sleepovers despite wet nights. More on this later.)

- **Protect privacy.** Place the chart on the inside of your child's bedroom door. The successes and setbacks are between you and your child only; there is no need to involve siblings or other children.

If you try an incentive program and after three weeks you see your child makes little or no progress, end it. Some children don't gain control through the night so easily.

Stories from the Bathroom

Stars for Success *(LanYing, 5 years)*

LanYing was dry about three nights a week; the other four nights she wet her bed. Her mom, Maryanne, reminded LanYing each night before bed to try to stay dry. On occasion, she'd get LanYing up during the night to urinate into the toilet. Sometimes LanYing would go and sometimes she was too groggy. Either way, LanYing continued to wet her bed several nights a week.

Maryanne decided to try an incentive program to help LanYing control her bladder every night. She placed a star chart on the back of LanYing's bedroom door. On the mornings she woke up dry, she received a star. After earning five stars, she could purchase a DVD to keep as her very own. If she had a nighttime accident, no stars were added and no stars were removed.

This was all the incentive LanYing needed. After three weeks, she trained herself to stay dry. Sometimes she'd wake herself up in the middle of the night to go to the toilet. The reward system helped her gain nighttime control.

For LanYing, a star chart was effective. Her body had developed to the point where she could hold in her urine all night—wetting the bed had only been a habit. The reward system provided the incentive to move from wet to dry nights.

STRESS

Many children wet their beds in response to the stress of change in their lives. Changes such as a new sibling, their parents' divorce, a death in the family, a new school, or a long-term house guest are all stressful. If your child is dry through the night and suddenly starts wetting, it's likely a sign of stress. Until the stress is relieved, or until the child has adjusted to it, the bedwetting will probably continue. Be understanding and don't panic—in time, your child will go back to dry nights.

If a child has been dry for six months and then repeatedly wets again, there could also be medical causes. Though this is uncommon, it's best to check with your doctor.

Stories from the Bathroom

Occasional Stress *(Pedro, 3½ years)*

Pedro learned to pee and poop in the toilet during the daytime just after his third birthday, but each morning his diaper was soaked. Six months later, his mom made this suggestion, "Pedro, I want you to try sleeping through the night without a diaper." Pedro agreed. It was amazing; the next morning Pedro woke up dry. Why? When the diaper was in place, it gave Pedro permission to pee. Without the diaper, he was aware of the need to hold in his urine all through the night.

Even though Pedro stayed dry most nights, he occasionally wet his bed until he turned eight years old. The wetting episodes occurred whenever there was a slight disruption in Pedro's life: a vacation, a friend over to spend the night, staying at Grandma's, or the start of school each year. For about a month after the beginning of kindergarten, first, and second grade, Pedro's bed was wet most mornings. Mom caught on to Pedro's pattern of stress-related bedwetting and was never shocked when it occurred. By third grade, these temporary wetting episodes disappeared.

AT FIVE YEARS

Most children learn to stay dry between ages three and five, though 15% still wet the bed at five years old (more boys than girls are in this group). In addition to what is suggested above, here are some other ideas to try.

Increase Child's Responsibility

Before breakfast, have the child dispose of or put the wet diaper/disposable where it belongs. One girl was seven before gaining night-time control. Between ages five and six, she slept in a slumber bag with a thin rubber sheet between the sheet and mattress; this simplified the laundry and bed changing process. It was her responsibility to put her slumber bag in the wash each morning. At six, she also added the soap and started the machine.

Measure and Hold

When children are home during the day, they may be interested in measuring their urine in a plastic measuring cup. Measuring increases awareness of the overall process and helps children focus. Teach them how to catch the urine while on the toilet and then how to dispose of it. (If you're worried about how sanitary this is, be aware that urine is normally germ-free.)

Wait

It is helpful for some children to wait as long as possible when it's time to urinate. Squeezing the muscles that hold the urine in causes the bladder muscle wall to relax so it can hold more urine. For a few children, this practice may even increase actual bladder capacity. Another way to learn control of the "holding" muscles is to start to pee, then squeeze and stop the flow. These are the same muscles that mothers exercise when doing Kegel exercises after childbirth. Hold for a couple seconds, two or three times per day.

Hypnosis

Starting after the fifth birthday, hypnosis, or self-hypnosis, can be effective for a number of children who struggle with bedwetting. Hypnosis provides positive suggestion when the mind is relaxed. If you're interested in this approach, you can try it yourself or work with a child therapist who does hypnosis.

A reputable book on this subject is *Raising your Children with Hypnosis* by Donald Mottin. The author points out that intention must be stated in the *present tense* and *positively* rather than negatively. The subconscious mind takes things quite literally. If you say "My bed will be dry," this could mean tomorrow or a year from now. So instead, you say, "My bed is dry." Furthermore, the mind works largely in pictures, so create a picture of what you *want*, not the opposite. Instead of, "I won't wet my bed," more effective suggestions are, "My bed is dry" or, "My bed stays dry every night."

Stories from the Bathroom

My Mind Will Wake Me Up *(Brian, 5 years)*

Five-year-old Brian really wanted to stay dry at night. He was afraid of getting teased at sleepovers. After hearing about self-hypnosis, his mother, Gail, sat down with him. She drew three roundish shapes to represent an empty *bladder, an* almost-full *bladder, and a* too-full *bladder.*

She then explained that during the night, everyone has times of light sleep when they can notice things (even though they are asleep), and times of deep sleep when they don't notice anything at all. "If your bladder gets too-full during deep sleep, it empties, and the bed gets wet."

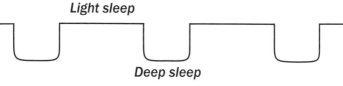

Light sleep

Deep sleep

—continued on next page

—continued from previous page

Then Gail drew a picture to show that Brian's mind would notice his almost-full bladder before *he went down into deep sleep.*

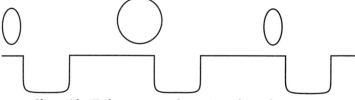

She said, *"Before you go down into deep sleep again, your mind knows when your bladder is almost full. If it is, then your mind wakes you up. You can go pee in the toilet, go back to bed, and wake up dry in the morning."*

That night at bedtime, Brian and his mom took some deep relaxing breaths together. Then they repeated several times out loud, "When my bladder is almost full, my mind wakes me up. I get up, pee in the toilet, go back to bed, and my bed is dry in the morning." Brian closed his eyes and repeated the lines several more times. Mom asked him to imagine how he would feel in the morning with his bed dry. He said he'd be happy! The next few nights showed no improvement, but Mom and Brian continued their bedtime lines. On the fifth morning, he woke up dry. He was delighted. Brian continued his nighttime self-reminders and his bed stayed dry from then on out.

PARENTAL REACTIONS

Unfortunately, some parents don't understand the physical and genetic causes of bedwetting and think if their child just tried harder, he could manage to stay dry all night long. They might accuse the child of not caring, being lazy, or believe their child is wetting the bed on purpose just to make them angry. Parents may be especially confused by a child who stays dry elsewhere, but wets the bed at home. In fact, such children may sleep more deeply at home and thus only have trouble with dryness there.

The most useful thing you can do is develop a plan to manage the problem, because, for many children, the most common remedy is time. Your child's body needs time to mature physically. He also needs reassurance from you that the problem *will* end.

AT SIX YEARS

If your six-year-old child climbs out of bed each morning with a wet diaper or wet pajamas and sheets, don't feel alone. About 12% of children continue to wet the bed after their sixth birthday. At age ten, 5% still have the problem of bedwetting. Some children do not gain control until puberty. At sixteen years, 1% still have a problem.

CONSULT YOUR PHYSICIAN

If your child is still wetting the bed after his sixth birthday, consult your doctor. Bedwetting after age six usually has a physical component. There are many reasons why a six year old might still wet the bed: slow physical maturation, urinating while deeply asleep, the bladder wall muscle remaining tense rather than relaxing to full capacity, a deficiency in antidiuretic hormone (ADH—discussed on page 152), persistent urinary infections, or occasionally, physical abnormalities in the urinary tract. Each of these physical components can be addressed with various techniques.

A six year old who consistently wets the bed also may be suffering emotionally from lagging behind others. Some parents are convinced their child is willfully wetting the bed. Whatever the situation, it's time to seek professional help. Start with your doctor.

MAINTAIN A POSITIVE ATTITUDE

In order to eventually achieve nighttime dryness, you must believe that, underneath it all, your child wants to stop wetting. Accept the fact that your child's body just isn't able to stay dry all night long.

It's important to notice how wetting the bed affects your child. Some children feel discouraged. They really try, but the problem persists. Your child knows other kids don't wet the bed, so why does it happen to him?

It's important to explain to your child that bodies are different. For example, tell your child there is probably a delay in his physical maturation; the needed connection between his bladder and brain is just taking longer to develop. Or, if your child is a sound sleeper, include this in your explanation. "You sleep so deeply, your brain doesn't get the message— or it ignores the message—that your bladder is full. Consequently, when your bladder is full, it simply empties by itself. Someday, when you're a little older, you'll wake up dry."

Try hard to set your emotions aside. Let go of the idea that your child doesn't care about the bedwetting or is wetting the bed just to irritate you. An angry or dispirited response from you will not change the situation. If your child physically cannot control the bedwetting and you expect—or even demand—he do so, he will feel ashamed, and his self-esteem will suffer.

AT SEVEN YEARS

There is a social expectation that children beyond the age of six years should not wet the bed. There are other developmental expectations people may hold for children past six: such as being able to read, swim, or ride a bicycle. The truth is children vary significantly as to when they achieve these milestones. Nighttime dryness is no different. A child's self-esteem suffers when parents and the rest of society hold onto rigid expectations regarding his developmental timeline.

Any teasing from siblings needs to be stopped. Here's all you need to say, "Sam wets the bed just like I did when I was a child. Someday he'll stay dry at night, but right now he can't help it. Teasing only makes Sam feel bad. He needs your understanding. I will not allow you to tease him."

WETTING ALARMS

Alarms, recommended by many pediatricians, are the most effective treatment for bedwetting for children ages seven to twelve (they generally don't work with younger children). Alarms are most effective when children are highly motivated, already have occasional dry nights, and have the necessary help from parents.

These alarms condition the child to respond to wetness. An alarm goes off with the first drop of wetness. There are many different sensors and alarms on the market at various prices. A sensor attaches to underwear or pajama bottoms. An alarm may attach to the wrist, to the pajama top, or sit across the room. When the alarm goes off, the child is supposed to hurry to the bathroom to finish urinating in the toilet. Eventually, the alarm alerts the child to signals from his bladder that he needs to pee. For many children, the alarm helps them attain nighttime control.[10]

Other children sleep right through the alarm. Remember that many children wet during the deepest stage of sleep. Once you've learned from the alarm when the wetting usually happens, wake your child 30-45 minutes earlier, when he is in a lighter stage of sleep. Encourage him to notice the sensations in his bladder and get to the bathroom at this earlier time in the night.

Parents are often eager to try this mechanical device, but its success is directly related to how highly motivated the child is to succeed and how much help the parents provide. Especially at first, the child needs help from his parents to get up in the middle of the night and go to the toilet. Don't expect your child to handle this by himself. Some parents find the process easier if they sleep in the child's room during the training period.

Once the child has been dry for 14 nights, remove the alarm. Many children will relapse one to several times before night training is really complete. With each relapse, return to the alarm; remove it after another 14 dry nights. The entire process often takes two to three months.

Encourage the child with stars along the way for each small step: waking up with the alarm, going to the bathroom, putting on dry clothes, and replacing the sensor.

Stories from the Bathroom

Dad Helps with Alarm *(Martin, 7 years)*

Jim was determined to help his son, Martin, overcome bedwetting by using a buzzer alarm. When the buzzer sounded, Jim got up, made sure Martin was awake, escorted him to the bathroom, and had him pee in the toilet. If Martin had already peed in his pajamas, Jim woke him up

—continued on next page

---

[10] To find an alarm, check with your doctor or try one of the following websites: www.bedwettingstore.com, www.pottymd.com, www.nytone.com, www.wetstop.com, www.nitetrain-r.com, or www.pottypager.com.

—continued from previous page

anyway. He wanted Martin to be aware of the fact that he had just peed in his bed. Sometimes he was so deep in sleep, Jim had to pat his face with a cold, wet washcloth to wake him up.

When Jim and Martin first started this program, they were up five times a night. Jim didn't yell or act exasperated; he just proceeded with extreme patience and discipline. His determination and discipline were eventually adopted by his son. After two months, Martin acquired enough control to sleep through the night without wetting his bed. Sometimes Martin got up during the night to pee, other nights he slept through the night, holding his urine until he woke up.

Not every parent can muster up the kind of discipline it takes to help a child during the night. Some parents become too sleep-deprived to remain calm in the middle of the night. If this is true for you, choose one of the other methods of managing bedwetting (such as teaching your child to handle his own laundry), and wait for his body to mature.

MEDICATIONS

If an alarm has not been successful after four to six months of really trying, medicines are useful in about 50% of children. One such medicine helps relax overly tense muscles of the bladder wall so it can hold more urine. Medications are generally effective only while they are being taken. They may lose their effectiveness if taken over time and may have uncomfortable or harmful side effects. Thus, they are generally not used on an ongoing basis. However, they may be helpful for sleepovers or summer camp. Which medicines are considered safe and effective changes over time. Check with your pediatrician for the latest information. If she does prescribe one, be sure to try it out at home first. Though these medications are occasionally prescribed for six, or even five year olds, they are generally not prescribed for children under five.

AT EIGHT YEARS

Enlist your eight year old's interest and cooperation to work on nighttime dryness. Realize that children at this age are likely to be discouraged. Work with your doctor as well. Continue to be supportive while you increase the child's responsibility and offer incentives. To increase awareness and motivation, stop using night diapers or disposables. Instead, use a waterproof bed pad. Offer a towel to cover the wet spot during the night or use two bed pads together so the top wet one can be easily removed. Do not carry the child to the bathroom at this age. Instead, wake him or use a wetting alarm so that he can walk to the bathroom by himself.

Stories from the Bathroom

Anger Doesn't Help *(Jacob, 9 years)*

First thing each morning, Kadi would check Jacob's bed for wetness. Her day would get off to a bad start if the bed was wet. She ranted and raved, "Why can't you just get up in the middle of the night and pee in the toilet? I'm so tired of all these wet sheets. Your room stinks and your friends won't want to play at your house because of the smell in your room."

Jacob just ignored his mom and this made her more exasperated. She was upset that Jacob didn't show any signs of disappointment or frustration regarding his wet bed. She wondered if he even cared about trying to develop nighttime control.

Finally, Kadi consulted a child development specialist. The specialist compared Jacob's bedwetting to children who get nose bleeds in the middle of the night. They don't feel it; they just wake up with blood on their pillow and wonder how it happened. If the problem persists, the specialist explained, a child learns to wake up to take care of it. Usually though, the nose bleeds eventually end on their own. Bedwetting is not that different. The specialist further explained that when toilet training (or bedwetting) becomes more important to the parent than to the child, the child shuts down any natural desire to progress further.

—continued on next page

—continued from previous page

Successful Sleepover *(Jon, 10 years)*

Jon and Tyree were best buddies in fifth grade. Tyree invited Jon to spend the night. When Jon's mom, Reagan, brought him over to spend the night, the boys ran upstairs to play. Reagan said, "Jon occasionally has an accident in the middle of the night. He has his sleeping bag and he can sleep on the floor. If he wets, he knows to roll up his pajamas and sleeping bag in the morning and put them in the storage bag. If it's not a problem for you, it's not a problem for Jon." Shareese replied, "It's not a problem for me."

The next morning no one knew or asked if Jon wet his sleeping bag. He simply managed the situation himself; his self-esteem and his friendship with Tyree remained intact.

—continued below

Another option for sleepovers is to pack a disposable diaper inside the sleeping bag before leaving home. Once the child is inside the bag and the lights are out, he can slip the diaper on.

—continued from above

Same Genes, Different Outcome
(Matthew, 12 years)

Tom wet his bed when he was a kid and suffered lots of teasing from friends and siblings. His mom and dad shamed and humiliated him. Tom's son Matthew was now wetting the bed. Painful childhood memories resurfaced in Tom. He was determined not to let Matthew suffer the embarrassment he experienced as a child.

—continued on next page

—continued from previous page

Tom told Matthew, I understand what you're going through. I know how hard it is to be the only one at a sleepover with a wet sleeping bag. Tom shared his childhood memories, offering lots of understanding and support to Matthew. He finished with the comment, "If those kids tease you about wetting the bed, then they're not really your friends."

With Tom as Matthew's most important ally, he had enough strength to understand and accept his bedwetting situation. He even developed enough confidence to explain it to others. By age twelve, he matured enough physically to remain dry through the night, but most importantly, his self-esteem was secure.

Here are some do's and don'ts to help your child progress toward nighttime dryness and preserve his self-esteem.

Do:

- **Do empathize** with your child, "I know you want to stay dry. Someday you'll gain control."
- **Do explain** that bodies develop at different rates in their ability to remain dry all night; for him, it's just taking longer.
- **Do reassure** your child that, in time, she will gain nighttime control.
- **Do reward** with a star chart incentive program, but if it isn't effective after three weeks, drop the plan.
- **Do plan** for an easy cleanup so your older child can manage mostly by himself.

Don't:

- **Don't label** your child a bedwetter.
- **Don't ask** each morning if your child wet the bed.
- **Don't let bedwetting dominate** your morning conversation. Don't constantly talk about it or call too much attention to the problem. Your relationship with your child is about so much more than that.

- **Don't assume** your child will show emotional distress about night-time wetting.
- **Don't act disappointed** or disgusted if you find a wet bed.
- **Don't humiliate, shame, or punish** your child for wetting the bed.
- **Don't compare** your child who wets the bed to other children, "Your three-year-old sister doesn't wet the bed—why do you?"
- **Don't allow teasing** by siblings.
- **Don't discourage sleepovers** because of the problem.

10

Constipation and Bowel Retention

Constipation and bowel retention are such personal subjects that people are often embarrassed and reluctant to bring up the problem with friends, family, parent educators, nurse practitioners, or even their family physician. These topics are, however, obviously important.

DEFINITIONS

For clarity, here are some definitions that relate to our discussion of the topic.

Normal Bowel Movements

Many people usually have a bowel movement once a day—the time may vary or be quite regular. A few people normally move their bowels two or three times a day. Still others go every two to three days. All of these patterns are normal as long as the stool is formed, yet soft, like toothpaste. Before you start teaching your child to have bowel movements in the toilet, notice how often he or she usually has a bowel movement. It's important to be aware of your child's natural pattern. When potty training, if your child maintains his or her usual bowel regularity, it is a sign that the process is going well.

Constipation

Constipation is difficult, or infrequent, movement of the bowel. It is a problematic delay. The longer stool stays in the large intestine, the more water is reabsorbed back into the body, so the stool becomes drier, harder, and more difficult to pass. Such dry stools may look like hard, little "rabbit pellets" instead of having the smooth, soft toothpaste consistency that is ideal.

Parents of children who constipate easily usually learn to watch their diets carefully. They also notice if a disruption in their child's schedule triggers constipation. For instance, travel, a simple change in the daily routine (such as going from two naps to one), or a more significant event, like starting child care, can all trigger constipation.

Bowel Retention

People automatically override the natural urge to empty the bowels when a toilet isn't available or when the timing isn't convenient. Some children carry this waiting to an extreme. When under stress, or in a power struggle around toileting, they may resist the natural need for days. Bowel retention may be a signal your child is not ready for training or is feeling overly pressured to use the toilet.

The problem with bowel retention is that it often becomes a negative cycle. Dry, hard stool can be painful to pass. To avoid pain the next time, the child delays longer and the problem gets bigger. At a certain point, the large stool stretches and weakens the intestinal wall. This, in turn, can damage nerves, so there is less "need to go" sensation for the child. Clearly, a vicious cycle can develop. The child avoids the toilet even more and the situation worsens.

Impaction

The stool becomes so hard, dry, and large that some form of medical help is needed in order for it to pass.

Soiling

If children retain their bowel movements up to six to nine days, uncontrolled, loose stool then leaks around the plug of hard, impacted stool. This leaking into the child's underpants results in soiling several times a day. When soiling occurs in children past their fifth birthday, the medical term for it is *encopresis*. Soiling can also be caused by stress rather than bowel retention.

Fiber

This is food that passes through the intestines without being digested, such as the woody cellulose covering of wheat, called wheat bran. Fiber swells up with water and therefore makes bowel movements larger, softer, and easier to pass. All children and adults need adequate fiber in their daily diets to maintain bowel health.

CAUSES AND PREVENTION OF BOWEL PROBLEMS

A child may not poop in the toilet for many reasons. In the process of toilet training, you want to do all you can to prevent constipation and bowel retention.

Those Most at Risk

Children who have a tendency toward constipation are often the first to begin to retain their stool if they feel stressed about the process of bowel training. If your child is prone to constipation, proceed carefully with toilet training. Be ready to relax and back off for a while, if needed.

Diet

Because of its high fiber content, wheat bran is an excellent natural stool softener. Look for whole grain breads and cereals or those with extra bran. Some children are allergic or sensitive to wheat. Other sources of fiber include oat bran, rice bran, peas, lentils, beans, apples, prunes, and raisins. Because cooking breaks down some types of fiber, *raw* fruits and vegetables are especially valuable sources of fiber. Cheese and processed foods, which are often low in fiber, can both contribute to constipation.

To keep stool soft, children also need sufficient liquid—water is the best option. Water provides liquid without extra calories and without harming teeth. If your child currently refuses anything but sweetened liquids, gradually (over the course of several weeks) dilute them with more and more water until your child becomes accustomed to the taste of plain water.

If your child is inclined toward constipation, it's especially important to provide a non-constipating diet that includes plenty of water. Children are getting enough water if their urine is generally light, "straw" colored, as opposed to dark, concentrated, and strong-smelling.

Exercise

Exercise affects overall well-being. It also increases muscle contractions in the bowel, so food moves through somewhat more quickly and stools have less time to become dry and hard. It's recommended that preschoolers have at least 60 to 90 minutes of exercise *per day*—much of that in free play.

Exercise should be fun; model an active lifestyle by playing actively with your kids. Running and climbing at the park, walking with parents, dancing, kicking balls, riding a tricycle or big wheel, jumping on a trampoline, playing in a wading pool—all of these activities are healthy for small bodies. Fours may begin to enjoy some jogging with adults. Active kids naturally move faster, though it's equally important that low energy kids also exercise at their own slower pace.

Child Not Ready for Training

Don't start toilet training too soon. Wait until the child is ready. Remember that most children today are trained somewhere between ages two and three and a half—girls usually before boys. Before you launch into bowel training, re-read the readiness signs listed at the end of Chapter 1.

Children usually learn to be bowel trained and urine trained separately. These are two totally different muscle sets to learn to control. So work on one at a time. Relax. Readiness for each may come at different times.

If your urine-trained child asks for a diaper when it's time for a bowel movement, go ahead and put one on. Bowel retention often occurs when a child is urine trained but requests a diaper for bowel movements. A well-meaning parent who wants the child to poop in the toilet (not in the diaper) refuses to grant the child's request and bowel retention follows. Since the child can't quite bring himself to poop in the toilet yet, he keeps the poop in for days. If this is the case with your child, your best response is to give him a diaper. Physically and intellectually he may be ready, but emotionally he just isn't ready to give up those diapers. In addition to giving out diapers when requested, establish practice sessions (see Chapter 3, pages 38–42) when the child is required to sit on the toilet, but not expected to perform.

Many children, once the diaper is on, squat to have a bowel movement. This is a natural position. When on the toilet, a footstool is important; it gives the child some leverage from which to push. The footstool may be more effective if it is high enough that the child's knees are slightly above the waist. Leaning forward can also help mimic the natural position.

Stories from the Bathroom

"Diaper, please" *(Brianna, 3 years)*

Between two and a half and three years old, Brianna urine trained quickly. But when she needed to poop, she said, "I need a diaper, Mommy." With her diaper in place, off she went to her bedroom for her bowel movement.

Melissa tired of this routine quickly and soon refused to give her a diaper, "No, Brianna, you need to poop in the toilet, not in a diaper. You're a big girl now. You pee in the toilet and you need to poop there too."

Brianna sat on the toilet for the longest time, but she couldn't relax and go. Three days went by with no success. Melissa worried about her daughter's physical well-being, so she agreed to put a diaper back on for bowel movements.

Melissa consulted the nurse practitioner at her doctor's office. The nurse reassured Melissa that putting the diaper on Brianna was the best approach, but also suggested two five-minute practice sessions on the toilet each day. Brianna was required to sit on the toilet— she could look at books or listen to music while she sat, but she had to practice. Taking time for these sessions helped Brianna adjust to the toilet; within two weeks, she was pooping there.

—continued on next page

—continued from previous page

In addition to the practice sessions, Dad and Brianna made brown play dough. Melissa purchased a play dough maker at the toy store—a contraption which seems to emulate a bowel movement. This play activity helped Brianna understand the pooping process, which, in turn, helped her eventually to overcome her reluctance to have a bowel movement in the toilet.

Although this example occurred with a girl, it is with boys that bowel retention occurs most frequently.

A Warning Sign

If your child usually pooped twice a day in a diaper and now, because of bowel training, is only going every other day, consider that a warning sign. He may not be ready yet, or may be feeling pressured. Lighten up and back off.

Negative Attitudes

When you're changing your child's diapers, don't act repulsed or disgusted with the natural process of elimination. If you are really bothered by the odor, breathe through your mouth (or in through your mouth and out through your nose) so the smell is less intense. Be glad your child is eliminating. If your child has an accident, don't say things like, "How can you stand that icky poop in your pants? It's dirty and disgusting." Just calmly clean the child and state, "Oops, you had an accident. It's okay. I know someday you'll poop in the toilet."

Anxiety

Parents may be too fastidious about cleanliness and unknowingly convey their discomfort with the whole natural process of elimination to the child. The result is a child who would rather not poop, wipe, flush, and wash hands and so retains her bowels to avoid all that trouble.

When your child is learning to use the toilet, provide lots of opportunities to play with dirt, mud, sand, and play dough. Purchase a play dough press at the toy store. This tactile play is therapeutic; children can come to terms with the process of elimination through this messy play experience.

Pressure and Power Struggles

As we discussed in Chapter 6, be careful not to get into power struggles over toileting. An emotional battle can result in your child refusing to use the toilet and retaining his stool. Remember, ultimate control lies with the child. It's his body; he's the one in charge. You can encourage, reward, influence, and motivate, but you can't force a child to poop. If parents become too controlling in the area of toilet training, the child may become determined that only he will control this bodily function and refuse to perform. If toileting has become emotionally charged, back off, give it a month or two, and then try again—this time, gently.

Some parents are too severe in their overall approach to guiding their child's behavior. If parents attempt to control or dominate the child's every move, it may become extremely important to the child that he alone controls his bowel movements. Bowel retention can result. Instead, give children reasonable control through choices (appropriate to the child's developmental age and ability) about clothing, food, friends, and toys. If children have *some* positive control in other aspects of life, controlling their bowel movements won't become so critical to them.

Too often parents go overboard trying to convince their child of the importance of pooping in the toilet. Although talking to your child about the importance of pooping is appropriate, *too much* talk is rarely effective when it comes to changing a child's behavior.

Individual Differences

Some children can sit and poop immediately. Others need to sit on the toilet for a few minutes in order to relax before they can let go. These children can have difficulty if family life is rushed. Make sure children have the time they need to sit and relax on the toilet when they feel the urge, even if you need to change your schedule to accommodate this time. It's a lot easier to be occasionally late than it is to cope with a child's bowel retention.

Some children are less aware of sensations both outside and inside their bodies. They may need help figuring out when they need to use the toilet. If their bodies are regular, a particular time of day may work well for them to sit on the toilet. It's not so easy with irregular bodies. Other children are highly sensitive to sensation. They may be very aware of body needs and anxious to get out of wet or messy diapers. However, some of these children are also greatly distressed by messy toileting accidents.

For some children, learning to poop in the toilet is stressful just because it's new. They will need extra time to practice without performing. Such children may find it particularly uncomfortable to poop at child care or school, in places where there are no doors to the toilet stalls, or in a shopping mall with unfamiliar or noisy toilets. These children may delay having a bowel movement as long as possible. Such reactions are more common in children who are, by temperament, cautious or slow to adapt. Practice sitting in a new place before they actually need to use a strange toilet. If the child can't poop in unfamiliar places, be sure to arrange time to relax on the toilet upon returning home.

Stories from the Bathroom

Getting Past "Diaper, please" *(Francisco, 4 years)*

Francisco still asked for a diaper each time he pooped. Mom knew that the feel of the diaper helped him relax and let go. She also knew that change was hard for him; she expected bowel training could take a while. Mom made her own plan and explained each step the day before starting it.

When he asked for a diaper, she put it on as usual, but had him sit, diapered, on the potty for about 30 seconds while they sang a short "potty" song. He then went to his closet (his preferred place) to poop in his diaper. After a week, she said he needed to stay in the bathroom while he pooped in his diaper. Next, she said she'd no longer fasten his diapers. After the potty song, he could hold his diaper in place. The next

—continued on next page

—continued from previous page

step was to put the diaper under *the potty seat, with everything else the same. Then Mom gradually made the potty song and sitting time longer.*

Six weeks after starting this process, Francisco was pooping on the diaper in the potty. From there, it was easy to skip diapers entirely.

Toilet Overflow *(Noah, 3 years)*

One day Noah was on the toilet having a bowel movement. When he flushed, the toilet overflowed. The erupting toilet and mess terrified him. Mom started to yell, "Get a plunger and a mop! Did you throw something down the toilet? How did this happen?" Mom's alarmed reaction, although understandable, increased Noah's overall anxiety.

After this traumatic experience, Noah refused to poop in the toilet. He began to retain his bowels for three or four days at a time. It wasn't a conscious response on his part; he just never wanted the episode to repeat itself. Delaying bowel movements to gain control over the situation was his unconscious solution.

Mom and Dad worried, but reasonably concluded it was most important for Noah to resume his regular bowel movements. So they suggested he use a diaper temporarily when he needed to poop. This was just fine with Noah.

Mom and Dad then encouraged their son to flush the toilet for them. Also, they put Noah's teddy bear on the toilet several times a day for a pretend bowel movement. His fear of the toilet slowly disappeared. Within a month, he was back to using the toilet.

HOME TREATMENT FOR MILD CONSTIPATION

Here are some things you can do for occasional, mild constipation.
- Make appropriate changes in diet and exercise (see pages 137–138).
- Do not encourage long, hard pushing because this can cause overstretching and tiny, painful tears in the rectal tissue around the opening. Instead, encourage relaxing on the toilet for five minutes,

several times a day.

- If there is pain due to small tears in the rectal tissue (generally these are not visible), put some petroleum jelly around the opening before and after using the toilet.
- Use play dough to illustrate that the strong muscles of the anus can squeeze and break stool into little pieces that are easier to pass. Encourage children to tighten and relax their fist around play dough, as well as consciously tightening and relaxing the muscles of the anus.

RESPOND GENTLY TO SOILING ACCIDENTS

It is important to respond calmly and gently to soiling accidents. Your child may not even realize he has leaked loose stool into his underwear. When soiling continues day after day, the child often becomes accustomed to the smell and fails to notice it. Don't ignore the soiling, but don't scold the child either. If you smell something amiss, either clean him up or help him clean himself up. Keep in mind that you want your child to take as much responsibility as possible for toileting. This includes cleaning himself up and changing his clothes after a soiling incident (assuming he's at least four years old and reasonably able to do so).

A soiling accident signals the bowel is full. Sit your child on the toilet so he can attempt to relax and pass the stool. Remember to stay calm and matter-of-fact. This attempt to poop in the toilet should not seem like a punishment. It's important not to punish or humiliate the child for something over which he has no control.

Do not allow siblings and friends to tease a child with a soiling problem. Stop the teasers immediately and explain the situation to encourage empathy rather than stigma. Here's all you need to say, "Jason leaked poop into his underpants. He can't help it. You are not allowed to tease him. Come on, Jason, let's change your clothes."

Soiling is a medical problem. If you haven't already consulted your child's doctor, do so without delay.

WHEN TO GET MEDICAL HELP

If your child is often constipated, continues to complain of painful bowel movements, or hasn't had a bowel movement for three to five days (that is, several days longer than his or her usual pattern), then it is important to seek help from a doctor who is understanding and knowledgeable on the subject. If your child has bouts of soiling, talk to your physician immediately.

Because constipation, bowel retention, and soiling are embarrassing and emotionally charged topics, parents are often reluctant to mention them to their doctors. Get medical help, nonetheless. Bowel problems are not something you can just ignore and hope will go away. Untreated, ongoing bowel retention can damage the colon and soiling can harm self-esteem. The child usually ends up being teased and feeling ashamed.

CLEARING THE BOWEL

When a child has an impacted bowel, the first step is to clear it. Work closely with your child's doctor during the process.[11] Depending on the situation, there are different ways to reach the goal. Here are some remedies doctors may recommend.

Stool Softeners and Lubricants

Stool softeners are medicines that cause more moisture to be retained in the stool, making it softer and easier to pass. Mineral oil, a lubricant, makes the stool more slippery. Refrigerate mineral oil—it tastes better cold. You can mix some in with your child's fruit juice.

Laxatives

These medicines make the intestinal muscles contract more strongly than usual to push the stool out. They may be given by mouth or slipped directly into the rectum (suppositories). Laxatives are not recommended for regular use because the muscles can become less able to work on their own. (For children with certain disabilities who *can't* use their abdominal muscles to help push, laxatives may be a necessary part of their routine bowel program.)

---

[11] The American Academy of Pediatrics recommends you always consult your doctor before using over-the-counter remedies to treat constipation.

Enemas

Water (often with laxatives) is put directly into the rectum to loosen stool and causes the bowel muscles to contract.

After the impaction has cleared, your child will need plenty of water to drink and a non-constipating diet. She may need stool softening medicine for many months. The longer the colon has been overstretched, the longer it takes to recover. Follow your doctor's recommendations regarding medication and diet. If the child starts to get constipated again, check back with your doctor. If mineral oil is recommended long-term, it can cause vitamin deficiency. Ask about a daily vitamin supplement.

There may be need for emotional recovery as well—if there has been too much pressure around toilet training or if the child has felt painfully shamed or embarrassed about soiling. A child therapist can be a great help here.

CONSISTENT DAILY PRACTICE SESSIONS

Children who have had an impacted bowel for a long time often lose the natural urge to defecate due to nerve damage. Practice sessions provide an opportunity for the child who isn't feeling the urge-to-go signal. Establish a routine for Poo-Poo Times several times each day (even if she doesn't feel the need to go). During the practice sessions the child should sit on the toilet for two to five minutes of practice, or until a bowel movement is passed, whichever comes first. Although the best time for results is often about 25 minutes after a meal, you can also think back to what your child's natural pattern was before the difficulty began.

Accompany your child for these sessions on the toilet. Read or tell a story. You want this time to be relaxed, rather than a source of tension. Play some music, give the child a toy to manipulate as she sits, and then demonstrate and encourage actions to push out a poop. Keep this time positive and upbeat. It is important to find a time for toilet sitting that is convenient for you, because your child needs your positive involvement and attention. Don't start this potty-sitting time as an afterthought as you're rushing out the door in the morning. Eventually, your child will no longer need your company.

If your child attends child care or school, it's important to get the teachers on board. They need to allow your child to go to the bathroom *whenever* the urge strikes, without waiting for permission. Be sure to also keep a change of clothes at school.

Stories from the Bathroom

Dislike of Bowel Movements *(DeAndre, 18 months to 3 years)*

When DeAndre turned 18 months old, his mom, LaVon, placed a little potty chair in the bathroom. This was the same time frame she had used with her daughter, who quickly learned to use the toilet just after her second birthday. LaVon's success with her older child gave her experience and confidence.

LaVon was doing nothing more than acquainting DeAndre with the potty chair. She knew he was too young to train. She just wanted to familiarize him with the process. At first, DeAndre liked the potty chair. He'd sit there and chat with his sister as she took a bath. Then, inexplicably, DeAndre began to dislike the potty chair and even avoid the bathroom.

At his age, DeAndre was not a child easily coaxed into doing anything from getting into a car seat to going to bed at a reasonable time each night. So it wasn't too surprising when he started showing signs of resisting toileting. He was also fussy about being clean. He wouldn't play in sand or dirt and frequently washed his hands. Not surprisingly, he began to avoid the whole messy process of pooping in the toilet.

As DeAndre approached his second birthday, he started holding in his bowel movements. The most drastic stretch of time was six days. That's when LaVon called the doctor, who prescribed a baby laxative. The miserable feeling in DeAndre's system before taking the laxative, and the sensation as the laxative went to work, reinforced DeAndre'snegative associations with the whole process of elimination.

Further recommendations from the doctor resulted

—continued on next page

—continued from previous page

in DeAndre taking one tablespoon of mineral oil each day. LaVon tried giving it to him mixed with chocolate milk. He refused to drink it. Then she tried mixing it with peanut butter and spreading it on bread. He could tell the peanut butter was different and refused to eat the sandwich. Finally, in desperation, she mixed the oil with a little cola in a tiny cup. DeAndre had never tasted soda pop before and drank it down without hesitation. The mineral oil eased the process of eliminating stools. There was no more pain when DeAndre tried to poop and there were no more stomachaches accompanied by bowel retention. Slowly, he lost his fear and distaste toward his bowel movements. By age three, things were going smoothly.

Special Medical Help *(Jonathan, 3 to 4 years)*

Jonathan was retaining his bowel movements—sometimes up to a week. His family received help from an Encopresis Clinic at their local children's hospital. After the impacted bowel was cleared, the clinic suggested daily medication plus a toileting schedule: the child was to sit on the toilet for five minutes, twice a day. He wasn't required to poop in the toilet; he was just encouraged to try. It took a year before he was on a normal pooping routine without the mineral oil or scheduled toilet-sitting times. Patience and a matter-of-fact approach from his parents were both key to ending the bowel retention.

Jonathan's mom made this statement regarding her son's problem with bowel retention and soiling, "I never thought my days would revolve around my child's pooping schedule. We were forced to slow our days down as he learned to poop regularly on the toilet during his practice sessions. It took many months until he was pooping on a regular schedule. As I look back, I don't know how we managed, but we did. I'm so relieved it's over."

This mom had to temporarily set her daily tasks aside to assist her child in changing his bowel habits. If your child has a similar problem, you may need to do this too. You will need medical advice, a plan, and lots of patience—for your child's sake.

CHECKLIST FOR DEALING WITH BOWEL ISSUES

☐ **Attitude.** Adopt a gentle, supportive, and patient attitude.

☐ **Diet.** Adjust your child's diet and liquid intake.

☐ **Medical Help.** Consult your child's doctor and follow her advice regarding constipation and bowel retention. Find psychological help when appropriate.

☐ **Practice.** Establish two practice sessions on the toilet each day. If there has been a lot of family stress around toileting, back off and return to diapers for a few weeks before instituting practice sessions.

☐ **Individual Differences.** Work with, not against, your child's temperament.

☐ **Support.** Enlist the support and cooperation of your child's teachers and caregivers.

IF YOU HAVE TROUBLE FINDING HELP

As recommended earlier, start by contacting your regular doctor or pediatrician. You can also contact your nearest Children's Hospital or the pediatrics department in a hospital that is affiliated with a university.

11

Early Training: Is That for Real?

In traditional cultures around the world (Asia, Africa, the Middle East, and Latin America), half the world's toddlers and preschoolers are already potty trained. Early toilet training means regularly peeing and pooping in the potty by sometime between nine and fifteen months of age. This fact has caught the attention of a number of modern American mothers.

In order for this book to be thorough and informative, we have provided early training information here, even though later training is the method currently used by almost all American families. Some of today's parents are interested in older, more natural, or intuitive, ways of parenting, of which the Family Bed is an obvious example. As with co-sleeping, early potty training is not for everyone. At the end of this chapter you will find a list of advantages and disadvantages to early training. If the method interests you, the following information will give you an idea on how to proceed.

IS IT POSSIBLE?

How is early training even possible, given all that has been said in earlier pages about the necessity of waiting for readiness? The answer lies in the difference between conscious and unconscious learning. Pass a spoonful of bananas in front of a hungry six-month-old baby and her mouth automatically pops open. This baby responds to the internal cue of hunger and the external cue of food. Yet it will be many, many months before this same little one learns to say, "Mommy, I want a banana," or climb up and take a banana from the tabletop herself. Both methods get food into a hungry tummy. The first response is unconscious and requires adult help. The second is a conscious and independent action. So it is with toileting. The learning can happen either unconsciously or consciously, depending on the age of the child.

HOW DOES IT WORK?

How does early training come about? It's a subtle interplay between baby and caregiver. Beginning sometime between two and six months, Mom pays careful attention to the baby's elimination patterns and the body signals that come just beforehand. Thus, early training requires attentive, physical closeness—most easily achieved by carrying the baby close to Mom's (or other caretaker's) body. Just before the baby is likely to let loose, Mom holds the baby in a particular position over the potty chair and makes a specific sound. The baby gradually learns to associate the special position and the sound with relaxing the relevant muscles. This conditioning is reinforced by a "don't soil the nest" instinct that develops early when babies are consistently clean and dry. Babies who are in diapers full-time disregard feelings of bladder and bowel fullness because no one responds to them.

We normally get the first sense of bladder fullness before it is completely full, so there is usually adequate time to get the baby in position. An early-trained baby can hold the muscles tight for a few minutes until the familiar position and sound occur. By the time babies can crawl, most can get themselves to a nearby potty when needed and use it. Obviously, they still need help with undressing, wiping, dressing, and hand washing. There are, of course, some misses along the way. Caregivers deal with those episodes matter-of-factly to preserve good body image and self-esteem.

POTTY TRAINING IN AMERICAN HISTORY

If early training is possible, why don't Americans do it that way? Actually, at one time, we did. In 1900, American babies were generally potty trained by 12 months. The huge job of washing diapers by hand motivated parents to train babies early. However, early training is quite labor-intensive for Mom. When washing machines became available in the 1940s, many mothers found diapers easier than paying careful attention to their baby's bowel and bladder signals.

In the 1950s, the age of training moved up to 18 months—at which time 90% of toddlers were trained. At the same time, advances in psychology also made it clear that harsh toilet training techniques (shaming, humiliating, and spanking) could have painful long-term effects on a child's emotional well-being. Psychologists encouraged American parents to lighten up and wait until *children* were ready to train.

When disposable diapers became available in the 1970s, the age of training rose further; most children remained in diapers until age two. Then highly absorbent, gel disposable diapers came onto the market in 1980. Most American parents now start training between 23 and 31 months. The majority of children finish potty training between ages two and three and a half years.

In the process of making the cultural shift to later training, educators put down the old method, saying that it only "trained mothers," and instead, applauded the independence of later learning. Negative attitudes toward early training are now decreasing as understanding grows.

NORMAL ELIMINATION PATTERNS

To train a baby early, you need to identify his bowel movement and urinating patterns. These patterns, of course, vary from baby to baby. Here are some general trends. Early on, the bladder isn't always a very effective reservoir (that is, doesn't yet hold much of the urine that drips constantly from the kidneys). Thus, in the early weeks, babies may pee up to 8-20 times per day. At around three months, the bladder begins to work more effectively and tends to hold urine while the baby is deeply asleep or sitting up. Thus, babies are more likely to pee upon waking and when taken out of a carry pack or car seat.

To improve nighttime sleep, the body makes a hormone (antidiuretic hormone) that directs the kidneys to make less urine during the night. In the morning, while this hormone is at lower levels, extra fluid is cleared from the body. Thus, babies may pee every 20-30 minutes in the morning and only every two to three hours in the afternoon. How often babies pee is also affected by their liquid intake, how hot it is outside, and sometimes by certain foods they eat. Pay attention to your own baby's patterns.

Filling the stomach often triggers bowel action, so early on, bowel movements often occur during nursing or within 10-20 minutes afterward. Bottle-fed babies commonly pass one to two stools a day. Breast-fed babies range from one to seven per day. (A small percentage of young babies go four to seven days in between bowel movements. Despite the length of time, these stools are still soft.) Starting between four and eight months, the large intestine becomes able to recycle water more effectively; it moves water from the bowel back into the body so most babies begin to poop only once or twice a day.

COMMON URINATING SIGNALS

Newborns may signal in a variety of ways that they are peeing or are about to do so:

- Get very still.
- Look very intent.
- Face may tense, frown, grimace, or pout.
- Eyes may twitch or eyebrows rise.
- May shiver, squirm, kick, arch back, or fuss.
- Abdomen may tense.
- May drip a few drops of pee before they really let go.
- May fuss while nursing or pull away from the breast.
- A boy's penis may get slightly larger or become erect or his scrotum may contract.

Young babies may signal they are about to have a bowel movement by:

- Passing gas.
- Making a grunt or grimacing.
- Getting red.
- Bearing down.
- Squirming.
- Spitting up.

Older babies may give the following signals:

- Make a particular sound.
- Pat or look at their bottoms.
- Look or gesture toward the potty chair.
- Throw food from high chair.

- Rub their noses.
- Mobile babies may climb into or out of your arms, or crawl to the potty.

Toddlers also have many common signals:
- Say a special word.
- Look down at their legs.
- Clutch between their legs.
- Pull off diapers or pants.
- Play with the potty chair.
- Whine.
- Ask to be picked up.
- Act silly.

PARENT CUES AND BABY POSITIONS

Parents make a "cuing sound" that teaches babies to connect that sound with what's going on in their bodies. Common cues for urine are "sssss" or "pssss," and for poop are "uh" or "unh." These cuing sounds mimic the actual sounds of the child urinating or bearing down to have a bowel movement. Use the cuing sounds whenever or wherever your baby eliminates. Eventually, if bladder or bowels are reasonably full, you will be able to make the cuing sound and your child will respond by performing on the potty. If you are teaching cues to a toddler, also use the cues whenever the child observes you use the toilet. Toddlers learn from copying, so this helps them associate these special sounds with others using the toilet as well.

A special position cues the body in an additional way. Picture a little girl squatting to pee. This is a natural position for urinating or having a bowel movement. To mimic this for a baby, you want the baby's back against your abdomen. Hold baby's thighs (one in each hand), knees slightly higher than hips, and slightly apart. (There must be some sort of receptacle under the baby to catch the pee or poop.) Then

Under-the-thigh hold

adjust your position so you are comfortable sitting or standing. Use the same one or two positions regularly to help baby make the connection.

For boys, use your finger to aim his penis down or lean forward to get the necessary aim.

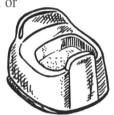

Once babies are able to sit on their own, you can use a special potty chair to achieve the position. These are stable, low potty chairs which are shaped to encourage this position of knees spread and raised slightly above the hips.

Stories from the Bathroom

The "Look" *(Ethan, 1 to 18 months)*

Christy was visiting China when she was pregnant and noticed that Chinese babies didn't wear diapers. She decided to give early training a try with her own infant son and began when he was about one month old. From the start, poop was easy to catch. Ethan usually pooped while nursing or immediately after, so she just held him over a plastic dish on her lap. She started holding him "in position" over the toilet while using the cuing sound when he was a few weeks old.

Grandma came to visit when he was three months old and thought Christy was kidding when she said Ethan could pee "on command." Christy took him to the bathroom, held him over the toilet, said, "Ssss," and he peed. Grandma was amazed.

At this age, he'd give Christy a particular look when he needed to go—a wide-eyed, surprised, "something's going to happen" look. At five months, he'd pat his belly when he needed to go. He couldn't hold the pee for very long after he signaled, so she had to get him to the toilet right away. Mom held him "standing" on the front rim of the toilet, leaning slightly forward. There were some accidents. Christy said she wouldn't recommend this approach for anyone who gets freaked out by pee or poop. By seven months, Ethan really didn't like being wet, so that helped motivate him to perform on the toilet.

—continued on next page

—continued from previous page

Once Ethan was crawling at 11 months, Christy would put him on the potty first thing in the morning. She put several interesting toys beside it during the night, so he was always happy to start his day sitting on the potty, playing with the toys.

In the winter time, when they were at home, Christy cut open the crotch seam of his pants, as they do in China, so it was easier for him to pee. By 18 months, he could pretty well manage toileting all on his own— except for wiping.

PARENT INTUITION

Some experienced moms learn to intuit when their baby needs to go. Intuition is a relaxed openness to thoughts or feelings. Some moms, who carry their babies a lot, feel sudden warmth on their body *as if* their child has peed. They respond to this intuition by putting the baby on the potty. This is very different from thinking obsessively, "Maybe she has to pee now!" and urging her to perform on the potty.

PARENT ATTITUDES AND EMOTIONS

If you are really bothered by the thought of pee on the floor and can't shift this mindset, early training isn't worth the stress for you or your baby. Today's early training is based on a responsive, nurturing relationship with the baby. It requires relaxed openness, a willingness to learn, patience, practice, and commitment. It also requires giving up the control that parents have with standard diapering—to change diapers at *adult* convenience.

If you are trying the early-training method and find yourself often worried about or upset by accidents, feeling competitive with other parents, or self-critical, back off. Similarly, if you often position and cue your baby with no results, take a break from early training.

THE PROCESS

Between two to six months, pay attention to your baby's eliminating signals and patterns. During these months, patterns usually become more predictable. Before babies are mobile, you can set them *on* a dia-per—rather than *in* a diaper—so you can see right away when she pees and what signs, if any, are present just beforehand. Of course, if it's a boy on his back, you'll put a light cloth over his body! Carrying your baby is another good way to increase awareness of body signals—the less cloth between you and the baby, the more obvious signals will be.

When to Start

Many parents start training at about three months because that's when babies begin to go for longer stretches between urinating. A few parents start cuing and catching at two weeks of age. Others aren't aware of the method until they have toddlers, so they proceed from there. Some-times early training is used only at home and not at child care or vice versa. All variations are workable, though babies will learn faster with consistency. What's most important is a comfortable, relaxed relation-ship with your child.

Cue the Baby

First, practice your cue. Whenever you see the baby pee or poop, make your cuing sound for as long as things are happening. (You can also make the cuing sound when you use the toilet yourself in the baby's pres-ence. Later, for toddlers, hold stuffed animals in position and cue them as well.) Then, using what you know about your baby's patterns and signals, as well as your intuition, put baby in position and say your cue.

Choosing When to Cue

Getting up in the morning is often a predictable time for your baby to urinate. Stay in position for one to two minutes, enjoying this pleas-ant time to snuggle. As you choose likely times and babies associate the position and cues with eliminating, they gradually learn to relax the appropriate muscles with the familiar sound and position. Babies who don't have to go may squirm, turn, or struggle. Don't insist. Some babies can be moved over the potty once they start to strain and grunt, but oth-ers are upset by suddenly being moved and then are unable to relax and go when they get there. Your best bet is to carefully observe his patterns and reactions and make your plans accordingly.

Lots of Things Can Stand in for a Potty Chair

What container do you use? You can sit with a yogurt carton between your legs, put a bucket on the floor, use a container on the bathroom counter, or sit on a stool facing the toilet. Some parents sit on the toilet itself and slide way back so there is space for baby in front.

Decide which positions work best for you and your child

Occasional Use of Diapers (or Not)

Given that the goal is a relaxed, confident relationship with baby, early-training parents use diapers when needed. For example, you can put a diaper on the car seat if you think you may get stuck in traffic. Until you are confident with signals, use a diaper when visiting a restaurant, your friend's house, or Grandma's carpeted front room. If your baby hasn't peed recently, you may want to put on a diaper when going for a walk. Some parents carry the familiar potty on outings instead of a diaper (or an appropriate container with a tight fitting lid). If your baby is used to a bare bottom, a long shirt or pants with a split crotch provide some modesty, as well as convenience, when out in public.

Provide Diaper-Free Time

Whenever you can be relaxed and comfortably attentive, such as outside or indoors (without carpets), let your baby have a bare bottom. Some parents are comfortable with a quick cleanup on the carpet, others are not. Try some diaper-free naps. If you're not too tired, cue the baby when you are awake after nursing at night. Your baby may stay dry for certain nighttime stretches. When you do use diapers, change the wet ones as soon as possible, so your baby becomes accustomed to feeling dry. Like other small creatures, babies (who are not in diapers full-time) develop a desire not to "soil the nest."

Provide a Potty Place

Once children are mobile, there are two potty options—being held by a parent over the toilet or potty chair, or crawling onto a solid, low, potty chair themselves. You may want to keep several around the house for easy access. So clothing doesn't get in the way, mobile babies and toddlers can wear a long shirt with leg warmers or split-crotch pants.

Stories from the Bathroom

Doing What Is Familiar *(siblings Mazel, 11 months & Yaffa, birth to 18+ months)*

Devorah was raised in Israel and was trained early herself. Her mother didn't have a washing machine and early training was common. When Devorah had her first daughter, Mazel, it seemed the natural way to train her. However, life was very busy and Mazel was in a child care center that wouldn't hear of early training. So Devorah didn't start using the method until her daughter was 11 months old.

She could tell from Mazel's face when she needed to go. She'd stop, get very still, and look self-absorbed. Signs for poop and pee were similar, except that pee was more subtle. Poops were easier to catch first. Like many early-trained babies, Mazel bowel trained first. Once she realized the potty was an option, she quickly learned to hold her urine and poop until Mom got her to the potty. She was pretty much trained in a week. When she was three, Mazel was diagnosed with autism. Other parents were struggling to train their children at that age and those children with autism had an even harder time. Devorah was thankful they'd already handled that issue.

With her second daughter, Yaffa, Devorah started early training at birth. She put her on a diaper, not in one, so she could see when she urinated. It was hard

—continued on next page

—continued from previous page

during the day while Yaffa was a newborn because she peed about every fifteen minutes. It got a lot easier around three or four months when she stayed dry for longer stretches.

While nursing, Yaffa squirmed and let go of the breast when she needed to pee or poop. Devorah would hold her in position over the potty, she'd go and then they would return to nursing. When she was sitting on Devorah's lap, or in the carrier, she'd bounce when she needed to go. In addition, Devorah cued her before bed and before they got in the car. Unless her bladder was pretty much empty, she'd relax and go.

At five months, Devorah put Yaffa in cotton training pants, without a plastic cover so she could see immediately if there was a miss. Once Yaffa could crawl, she usually went to the potty herself, lifted the cover, and used it. Between 12 and 15 months, the number of misses decreased dramatically. At 18 months, Yaffa missed pee only when she was intensely involved in something—about two or three times a week. She rarely missed a bowel movement.

Finding the Easy Way (siblings Maya, 8 to 22 months and Aruna, 1 to 18+ months)

Sabani planned to start potty training her daughter, Maya, around two years. But at eight months, Maya became constipated. Sabani's mother, who was from India, said "It's easier to poop in the 'natural' position." They had a very low potty chair that was shaped to spread the child's knees slightly apart, so the position resembled squatting. Sitting this way, Maya was able to poop more easily—which, in turn, eased the problem with constipation. So Sabani continued to use the potty to catch her bowel movements, which were quite regular.

At the same time, Sabani started putting Maya on the potty every one to two hours. She continued to use diapers in between these times, "Because I wanted my life to be easier, not harder," said Sabani. Around 15 months, she put Maya in pull up disposables. At 22 months, she took some extra time and switched her to panties full-time.

—continued on next page

—continued from previous page

With her second daughter, Sabani started catching poops around four months, just after nursing in the morning. Because Aruna was very regular, that was easy. Sabani put her on the potty often. Around 15 months, Aruna began to indicate she needed to use the potty by saying "Pee-pee." Mom often let her be naked around the house. If it had been a while since she'd used the potty though, Mom would try to keep her off the rug. At 18 months, Aruna only had occasional misses.

MANAGING MISSES

You can avoid misses by using diapers when you need them: during the early months, when you are under stress and cannot be attentive, when you need your sleep, when traveling and not yet confident, or when worried that a miss would be problematic.

Misses happen. Baby's ability to give clear signals can be thrown off by teething, illness, and constipation. Parental attentiveness can get interrupted by visitors, travel, marital discord, or a move. Communication can be thrown off with a different caregiver.

New stages of development also affect the process. Babies may suddenly shift to different signals. Things often backslide between eight and fourteen months when little ones get very focused on learning to crawl or walk. Independent toddlers may suddenly want to choose the potty place. Strong-minded two year olds may do better if you bring the potty to them or take the current favorite toy to the bathroom.

While most children push for independence around two and a half years, some intense toddlers do so as early as fourteen to twenty months. Many early trainers have potty training behind them by this time, but not all. Thus, there may be some overlap between the final stages of early training and an earlier-than-usual push for independence. In such cases, acceptance of misses (or the use of diapers) is important to avoid power struggles.

Once the process is well underway, parents may deal with one miss a day or once every few days. Some parents prefer cotton training pants (sometimes with an inner pad) to minimize wet spots, yet keep the process moving along. Your calm and accepting attitude is important here.

Hygiene Concerns

Many of us have been taught that urine is "dirty" or full of germs. In fact, pee normally has fewer germs in it than saliva. As pointed out earlier, some misses and accidents are inevitable. You need to be okay with this and calm about cleanup so as not to scare your baby. Every child deserves to grow up with a healthy attitude toward his or her body and the process of elimination. It starts in infancy with a parent treating this very personal area of the body with respect, gentleness, and a calm demeanor. This is true for all children regardless of the training method used—but it is particularly important when using early training because babies are more often without diapers while both Mom and baby are learning. If you find you can't be calm and matter-of-fact about occasional messes, then early training is probably not for you.

Stories from the Bathroom

Inconsistency Slows Progress *(Ashley, 4 months to 2 years)*

Kamala was from Tibet. Working in the United States as a nanny, it was natural for her to start training her young charge, Ashley, at four months. Kamala had the impression Ashley's parents didn't believe early training was possible and they certainly thought diapers were easier. At home on Saturday and Sunday, Ashley wore diapers. With Kamala during the week, she went without diapers and had to re-learn the signals and routines. From Monday through Wednesday, there were misses, but none on Thursdays and Fridays. When Ashley was two, her parents finally began to encourage using the potty on weekends at home. She quickly became trained full-time. Kamala reported training this way took much longer than it did in Tibet, where everyone used the same method.

NIGHTTIME TRAINING

Many babies don't pee at all while asleep, but rather during brief periods of wakefulness at night. Some early trainers even try to crawl off the bed in order to get to the potty. Many early-trained babies are dry at night before later-trained babies are dry during the daytime. This may happen because the early-trained babies have practiced daytime control for months and tend to get the hang of nighttime control sooner. On the other hand, some early-training families routinely use diapers at night to maximize sleep for parents.

Stories from the Bathroom

Two Nighttime Training Examples

Ethan's mom reported that in the early months, she used a water-proof liner or towel under him on the parental bed at night. She would put him on the potty when he woke up to nurse, but there were a lot of accidents. Eventually, she switched to nighttime diapers. He no longer needed them by 18 months.

Another mom said that her daughter slept with her from the start. When Mom felt the baby start to thrash her legs, she held her in position to pee and then fed her. Her baby was nighttime-dry by five months.

RETURNING TO WORK

Even if your child will be in child care where early training is not practiced, you can still practice catching pee and poop, cuing, and watching for signals when you are home. This will likely increase awareness and ease the process when your child is ready for regular, full-time training.

TRAVEL

Many families use diapers until they are comfortable with cuing. When they travel, they hold and cue a baby over a public toilet, or carry a diaper over which they can simply hold the baby. A container with a tight lid can work in the car. You can try cuing before leaving home and upon returning. Carry baby's potty for use in the car or at a friend's house. If you are going out where an accident would be a problem, you can simply put baby in a diaper.

THE END POINT

As with later toilet training, children are very different. Those who have higher body awareness, communication ability, and focused attention will progress faster than age mates with either method. For some babies, the process comes together in a surprising few weeks. More commonly, it's a number of months. Many use the potty consistently by a year. Sometimes there is regression due to illness or family stress. Sometimes toddlers simply stop signaling or responding to cues for a few months while they concentrate on other developmental issues. Most are quite consistent by 15 to 18 months, though a few are age two or older.

IS EARLY TRAINING FOR YOU?

Parents who have tried early training find a number of advantages to the early learning method.

Potty Training Is Finished Earlier

With the early-training method, potty training is usually complete much earlier—sometimes by 12 months, more commonly by 15 to 18 months, and almost always by two years.

Close Connection to Baby

The attentiveness that is required feels like a natural extension of the intimate, responsive connection with one's baby. Mothers who carry their young infants close to their bodies more easily notice the body movements that precede elimination.

A More Direct Route to the Goal

Sitting in wet or poopy diapers teaches babies to disregard their natural body processes and the sensations associated with them. Later, they will have to learn to pay attention to the sensations and what they mean all over again. Some preschoolers (especially those who find change difficult) will have trouble relearning how to relax and poop with a bare bottom—something babies don't find an obstacle.

The Cost
Early training saves money. Over the years, diaper service or disposables can add up to two to four thousand dollars per child.

A Greener Way to Potty Train
Each year 22 billion disposable diapers go into our landfills. Early training dramatically reduces the use of diapers.

Avoids or Solves a Diaper Issue
Diapers are difficult for some children. Early training avoids problems like:
- recurrent diaper rash.
- a baby bothered by diapers that must be snug.
- a baby who hates being changed.

Sidesteps Conflict or Power Struggles
Unfortunately, conscious control of bladder and bowel muscles usually develops around the time of a two year old's big push for independence. This can be a setup for power struggles. With early training, the process is usually complete before this common stage of resistance.

There are also disadvantages to the early-training method.

More Attention and Less Flexibility
Learning baby's subtle cues takes time and attention. Some babies can be successfully cued by parents after meals and naps. Usually however, it's essential to watch and feel for baby's signals more frequently than that. This requires being very close, most of the time. Since standing by the crib and watching for hours isn't practical, parents find it easier to carry their babies in order to feel the wiggles or squirming that indicate the need to go. While diapers can be changed at adult convenience, early toileting requires that adults arrange their schedule around the baby's toileting needs.

Need for Participation and Cooperation

It's usually the mom (assuming she spends the most time with the baby) who figures out the baby's patterns and then teaches them to the other adults. The toileting process will be much easier to accomplish if all who care for your baby are willing to learn, pay attention, and participate. This includes your partner, child care provider, babysitters, and anyone else who spends regular time caring for your baby.

If your partner or caregiver is opposed to early training, you can still proceed, though the process will likely take longer. In this, as in other areas of child rearing, it's important to work out compromises for a smooth-running household.

Returning to Work

Many American mothers return to work when babies are between three and six months of age—just when early training is really getting going. (However, if your child care provider is from an early-training culture, this is not a problem.)

PARENT TIME AND ATTENTION

The investment of parental time in training is also important to consider and compare. Training an infant takes more attentive time than training a toddler or preschooler. However, keep in mind that most parents change diapers for years before standard training starts. Therefore, the combined time of changing diapers and later potty training adds up to more parental time in total.

Another factor is the closeness and attentiveness involved in early training. A lot of holding is the easiest way to develop the close connection necessary for early training.

Task	Early Training	Later Training
Adults change (padding) or diapers regularly:	3-6 months	22-50 months
Active learning/training (zone of possible misses/accidents):	Signals and cuing: 6-15 months	Practice time: 1-4 months
Help needed to wipe after poops:	Up to 4-5½ years	Up to 4-5½ years

Only you can assess whether early training is right for your family. Be assured that both early and later training are safe and time-proven methods of potty training. Do what is right for your child and your lifestyle.

THE FUTURE

Will mainstream America embrace early training? Some educators believe this method will only appeal to a small group of *extreme* parents. Many others believe it may be the beginning of a groundswell movement like the ones that brought breast feeding and co-sleeping back to the forefront of parenting practices between 1960 and 1990. Time will tell. In the meantime, it can be interesting and valuable to learn how other cultures accomplish the important task of potty training.

MORE INFORMATION

See the Resource section for suggested reading, specifically, *The Diaper Free Baby* by Christine Gross-Loh and *Diaper Free* by Ingrid Bauer. For Internet information, try these search terms: Elimination Communication (EC) and Natural Infant Hygiene (NIH). There are internet support groups at www.diaperfreebaby.org and http://groups.yahoo.com/group/eliminationcommunication.

LOOKING BACK ON POTTY TRAINING

Nowhere are individual differences more apparent than in potty learning—differences in how parents teach and in how individual children learn. Some children progress quickly and smoothly through the process, while others will move in fits and starts. As in all aspects of children's growth, we are constantly reminded that it is a two-way street. We learn from them and they learn from us in the dance of a growing relationship. The good news is that they will learn to be potty trained and the family will move on to focus on other aspects of daily living.

When training is complete, look back and reflect. How did you go about the process? What techniques helped you succeed? Which steps were ineffective? It will be interesting to notice if your child masters other developmental milestones—reading, bike riding, swimming—in much the same manner. What did you learn about your child as you guided her toward toileting success? What did you learn about yourself as a parent? Your own stories from the bathroom will be a testament of growth and learning for you and your child.

Resources

Books for Parents to Read to Children

Cole, Joanna. **Your New Potty,** New York: HarperCollins, 1989. *A straightfor-ward story line provides children with a clear idea of how girls and boys go from diapers to using the potty chair. Photographs.*

Frankel, Alona. **Once Upon a Potty,** Ontario, Canada: Firefly Books, Ltd., 2007. *A story about a child who goes from peeing and pooping in diapers to using the potty. This book shows the child's body parts and illustrates bowel movements and urinating. There is a version for boys and one for girls.*

Galvin, Matthew. **Clouds and Clocks,** Washington, DC: American Psychological Assoc., 2006. *Too long and complicated for preschoolers, but appropriate for school-aged children who soil their underpants. An important book.*

Gomi, Taro. **Everyone Poops,** Brooklyn, NY: Kane/Miller Publishers, 1993. *Children are interested in most natural phenomena, including bowel movements. This book tells about animal poop and its different shapes, colors, and smells. The book concludes with, "All living things eat, so everyone poops."*

Holzwarth, Werner and Erlbruch, Wolf. **The Story of the Little Mole Who Went in Search of Whodunit,** New York: Harry N. Abrams, 2007. *Children enjoy this fun story about a mole who got pooped on and his search for the culprit "whodunit."*

Lansky, Vicki. **KoKo Bear's New Potty,** Minnetonka, MN: Book Peddlers, 1997. *KoKo Bear gets a potty chair, gets underpants, has accidents, and is finally successful. On each page there are tips and information for parents.*

Lewison, Wendy Cheyette. **The Princess and the Potty,** New York: Simon & Schuster, 2005. *An appealing story with a fairy tale quality about a princess who refuses to use the potty. When she wishes to wear pantalettes like the queen, she becomes motivated.*

Markes, Julie. *Where's the Poop?* New York: Harper Festival, 2004. *A simple, nicely-illustrated, lift-tab book which shows where animals (and people) leave their poop.*

Mills, Joyce and Crowley, Richard. *Sammy the Elephant and Mr. Camel: A Story to Help Children Overcome Bedwetting,* Washington, DC: American Psychological Assoc., 2005. *Sammy the elephant gradually learns to control his body as he grows and develops. If your child wets the bed, this book will help him understand the situation while building self-esteem.*

Munsch, Robert. *I Have To Go!* Toronto, Canada: Annick Press, Ltd., 1992. *A cute story about a common dilemma. Mom and Dad ask the child if he needs to use the toilet before climbing in bed, getting in the car, or going outside. He always says, "No!" but soon needs to go.*

Pinnington, Andrea. *Big Girls Use the Potty* and *Big Boys Use the Potty,* New York: DK Publishing, 2005. *Board books for young toddlers that use photographs and a simple rhyming story to show a teddy bear, then a child, use the potty.*

Rogers, Fred. *Going to the Potty,* New York: Penguin, 1997. *This book shows children how they change and grow in many ways, including urinating and having bowel movements in diapers and then in the toilet. Photographs of children illustrate the book.*

Sears, William, M.D., and Sears, Martha, R.N. *You Can Go to the Potty,* Boston: Little, Brown and Company, 2002. *This book is impressively clear, simple, straightforward, and positive—cute family illustrations. Suitable for boys or girls. Includes sidebars with details of interest for parents or older kids.*

von Konigslow, Andrea Wayne. *Toilet Tales,* Toronto, Canada: Annick Press, Ltd., 1991. *This charming, simple story explains why various animals don't sit on the toilet. The book ends with the line, "Toilets are meant for big kids like you."*

DVDs for Children

If children are three years or older, and especially if they don't have other children to watch, DVDs may be useful. Many are available—some based on the above books. Here are two we find helpful.

Elmo's Potty Time. Sesame Street, 2002. *In true Sesame Street style, the pro-*

gram is positive, tuneful, interesting, and covers an array of related topics. Nice section on identifying body cues.

Potty Power for Boys & Girls. Consumervision, 2004. *Covers the basics with songs and information. Emphasizes the goal of growing up, but unlikely to be helpful if a younger child is getting diaper-time attention from parents.*

Books for Parents

(Parents are oftentimes curious about toilet training books that promise quick or easy results. We include this first book to give you an idea of its content.)

Azrin, Nathan and Foxx, Richard. **Toilet Training in Less Than a Day,** New York: Simon & Schuster, 1989. *Parents are instructed to push liquids and salty foods during toilet training. Children are encouraged to practice running to the bathroom from different places in the house. The program is intense and may produce temper tantrums and resistance to toilet training.*

Bauer, Ingrid. **Diaper Free: The Gentle Wisdom of Natural Infant Hygiene**, New York: Penguin, 2006. *A detailed look at early training with pictures of positions and easy alternatives for equipment.*

Bennett, Howard J., MD., FAAP. **Waking Up Dry,** Elk Grove Village, IL: American Academy of Pediatrics, 2005. *In workbook format, this book is geared to helping parents and school-age children work together toward dry nights.*

Brazelton, T. Barry. **Toddlers & Parents,** Rev. ed., New York: Dell, 1989. *Offers parents a clear idea of what it's like to toilet train a toddler. The story of a little boy explains the trials and triumphs he experiences as he reaches this developmental milestone. Information about the inner developmental life of the toddler is included.*

Gross-Loh, Christine. **The Diaper Free Baby,** New York: HarperCollins, 2007. *Explains the process of early training in detail, with adaptations for starting with older babies.*

Lansky, Vicki. **Toilet Training,** 3rd ed., Minnetonka, MN: Book Peddlers, 2002. *A quick guide to toilet training. Offers a lot of tips from parents: what worked, what didn't. Photographs of various potty chairs and seats.*

Leach, Penelope. **Your Baby & Child,** 3rd ed., New York: Alfred A. Knopf, 1997. *You'll find a short section on toilet training in this information-packed book about baby and child care. Sensible and practical.*

Mack, Alison. **Dry All Night,** Boston, MA: Little, Brown & Co., 1989. *This book* *has two sections. The first is for parents and the second is for school-age children who wet the bed to read alone. Encourages kids to take complete responsibility for the situation.*

Mack, Alison. **Toilet Learning,** Boston, MA: Little, Brown & Co., 1983. *The first section is for parents and the second section is to be read aloud to children. The author gives a broad perspective on the toileting process and warns parents not to miss the period of peak readiness.*

Mottin, Donald J. **Raising Your Children with Hypnosis,** Bridgeton, MO: National Guild of Hypnotists, Inc., 2005. *Offers theory and practical application of hypnosis for common childhood issues, including bedwetting. Easy, non-technical language.*

Pantley, Elizabeth. **The No-Cry Potty Training Solution,** New York: McGraw Hill, 2007. *Deals with a wide array of practical issues that are often not covered in other books.*

Rapp, Doris, M.D. **Is This Your Child? Discovering and Treating Unrecognized Allergies in Children and Adults.** New York: HarperCollins, 1992. *Describes the elimination diet that allows parents to detect food sensitivities or allergies that may affect bedwetting.*

Schaefer, Charles, M.D. **Toilet Training Without Tears,** Rev. ed., New York: Penguin, 1989. *Dr. Schaefer not only offers a plan for toilet training but includes valuable information for children who are frequently constipated, retentive, or suffer from encopresis. If your child is over three and a half and resistant to urine or bowel training, be sure to read this book.*

Schmitt, Barton. **Your Child's Health,** 3rd ed., New York: Bantam Books, 2005. *In this complete guide to children's health issues is a section on toilet training. A list of Do's and Don'ts to prevent problems is included, as well as a section on children who resist training. Valuable reading if your child is constipated or retaining bowel movements.*

Van Pelt, Katie. **Potty Training Your Baby,** 2nd ed., New York: Avery Publishing Group, Inc., 1988. *Advises parents to "Start as soon as a baby is able to sit up on his on own and remain sitting for a good while without support." Valuable for its good advice regarding a pleasant attitude and frame of mind when it comes to toilet training.*

Wolraich, Mark L., M.D., FAAP. **American Academy of Pediatrics Guide to Toilet Training,** New York: Bantam Dell, 2003. *Clear, supportive, and medically accurate.*

Websites for Parents

Bedwetting alarms: www.bedwettingstore.com, www.pottymd.com, www.nytone.com, www.wetstop.com, www.nitetrain-r.com, and www.pottypager.com

Support groups for early potty training: www.diaperfreebaby.org and http://groups.yahoo.com/group/eliminationcommunication

Index